ACCOMPLICES TO ILLUSION

Poems

By

R. N. TABER

"Colour, creed, sex, sexuality…these are but part of a whole. It is the whole that counts."

First published in Great Britain in 2007 by Assembly Books, C-Hammond House, 45a Gaisford Street, London NW5 2EB.

All rights reserved. No part of this publication may be reproduced, stored in any retrieval systems or transmitted in any form or by any means without prior (written) permission of the author

Copyright 2007

ISBN 0-9539833-4-X; 978-09539833-4-6

Printed by PrintOnDemand, Graphic House, 1, First Drove, Peterborough PE1 5BJ

Also by the author:

Love And Human Remains: poems - Assembly Books, ©2001 (ISBN 0-9539833-0-7).

First Person Plural: poems - Assembly Books, ©2002 (ISBN 0-9539833-1-5)

The Third Eye: poems - Assembly Books, ©2004 (ISBN 0-9539833-2-3)

A Feeling For The Quickness Of Time: poems Assembly Books, ©2005 (ISBN 0-9539833-3-1)

Blasphemy: a novel – GLB, San Francisco; Gazelle Book Services, Lancs. ©2006 (ISBN 1-879194-61-9)

CONTENTS

DEDICATION
Autobiography Of A Beach   i

PART 1: *ACCOMPLICES TO ILLUSION*

Accomplices To Illusion	2
Back To Nature	3
A Common Garden Snapshot	4
The Bridge	5
Rediscovering Climate Change	6
A Nature Lover's Dream	7
Agenda For A Cull	8
The Squirrel	9
Spring Is A Girl In A Blue Print Dress	10
Summer Is A Man In A Blue Denim Shirt	12
Autumn Is A Man In Red	14
Winter Is A Woman In White	16
Lines On Nature Conservation	18
Pond Life	19
A Walk In Blean Woods	20
In The Company Of Dolphins	21
A Feeling For Seagulls [i]	22

The Horse Whisperer	23
Eternity Revisited [ii]	24
A Feeling For Spring	25
Swan Lake	26
Beating Up The Planet	27
Rear Window	28

PART 2: *WHATEVER HAPPENED TO LOVE?*

Whatever Happened To Love?	30
Bonding With Eternity [iii]	31
Love Endures	32
One Day	33
The Rose Lover	34
Weathering Love	35
The Zen Of Flower Arranging	36
No Handouts	37
Separate Stones	38
Secret Love	39
Rummaging The Archives [iv]	40
Night Watch	41
Too late For Poetry	42
Covenant With Love	43
Open Window	44
Sunny Days, Passing Storms	45
At Freedom's Call	46

Misty Memories [v]	47
Beauty And The Beast	48
Last Call	49
Making Up For Winter	50
Politics Of The Heart	51
Pink In The Frame	52
Shifting The Burden	53
Curtain Rising [vi]	54

PART 3: *DIRTY DANCING*

Private Lives	56
Dirty Dancing	57
Going For Broke	58
No Strategy For Surrender	59
Obsession	60
Fat Under Fire [vii]	61
Open Road [viii]	62
Coming, Ready Or Not	63
Regret	64
The Rhetoric Of Mortality	65
Spoilt For Choice	66
The Voice	68
Testament To Life	69
A View From the Edge	70
Signing Up With Ahab	71

Contract For Life	72
In The Blink Of An Eye	73
Time Spent In A Valley	74
Beyond Glastonbury	76
Dancer At The Edge Of Time	77
Ode To A Homophobe	78

PART 4: GAY IS OK, SAYS WHO?

Gay is OK, Says Who?	80
Let The Music Play [ix]	81
No Storybook Hero	82
Spring, On Cue	83
Postcards From the Edge [x]	84
First Christmas	85
Three Little Words	86
Confessions Of A Sandman	87
That First Time	88
Street Kisses	89
A Song For Gay Lovers [xi]	90
Genesis	91
Sometimes	92
Being Gay, Being Straight	93
Beloved Invader	94
A Christmas Blessing	95
Gay Sonneteer	96

Fast Tracking	97
Bring Me The Head Of An Honest Man	98
Living Over the Pawnbroker's Shop	99
Jack-In-The-Box	100
Mirror, Mirror	102
Life-force	103
Nothing Ever Quite The Same Again	104
Ode To A School Cap	105
A Christmas Story	106
Who Hasn't Heard The Fat Lady Sing?	107
Lines On Immortality	108

PART 5: *HALLOWEEN LANDSCAPE*

Halloween Landscape	110
Out Of Eden	111
Time And Again	112
The Rhetoric Of Blame	113
Now Iraq, What Next?	114
Pointing To Armageddon	115
Years On	116
Home Grown	117
Listening For The Dodo	118
Katrina's Wake	119
Once, New Orleans	120
Maelstrom	121

Long Winter, Lonely Spring	122
Soldiering On	123
A Stitch in Time	124
Red	125
Waiting For Rain	126
Cry, Wolf	127
Waking Up To Godot	128
Touchlines	129
Reflections On A Wet Night	130
God's Metaphor	131
Nature's Way	132
Last Stand	133
Come Twilight's Sword	134

PART 6: *BUSINESS AS USUAL*

Business As Usual	136
Customer Care [xii]	137
Witness For The Prosecution	138
The last Long Hauler Out Of E-Bay	139
Sounding Out The Stock Market	140
Caught On CCTV	141
House And Garden	142
Metamorphosis	143
Fundamentals	144
Game Over	145

Extracts From A Prison Diary	146
Making A Start	148
Just Another day In The Terror Business [xiii]	149
John Bull's Midnight Garden	150
A Crying Shame	151
Hurt Pride	152
The Rhetoric Of Separatism	153
A Predatory Life	154
Poor Sparrow	155
Suggestions	156

PART 7: *A KINDNESS OF GHOSTS*

A Kindness Of Ghosts	158
Proof Of Life [xiv]	159
In Black Satin	160
Every Poem Begs A Story	161
Extract From A Poet's Autobiography	162
What's In A Name?	163
Spring Cleaning	164
Among Wolves	165
Beyond Christmas	166
Listen With Mother	167
The Guardians	168
Last Exit To Erewhon	169
In Despair	170

Hope Is A Woman	171
Fairytales Are An Endangered Species	172
Looking For Africa	173
Ghost Fingers	174
Party Tricks	175
Handfuls Of Dust	176
Living With Ghosts	177
Among Slaves	178
Spring Sunshine	179

APPENDIX I

Welcome To The 21st Century	180

APPENDIX II

The L-Word	181

NB Except where indicated otherwise, the poems above were written between June 2005-March 2006. [Numerals beside poem titles refer to endnotes at the back of the book]. - RNT

ACKNOWLEDGEMENTS:

I would like to thank all those editors and publishers who have included my work in various poetry magazines and anthologies since I first began submitting for publication in 1993. I would also like to thank friends and colleagues for their support. A special thank you to Internet friends and contacts, many of whom I have never met in person; their Instant Message comments and e-mails have provided encouragement and inspiration since I first went online in 1998 and, hopefully, will continue to do so.

Roger Noel Taber

DEDICATION

AUTOBIOGRAPHY OF A BEACH

Sun and moon, sailing fickle skies
to safe harbours;
Sea, like a cabbage-stained tablecloth
edged with white lace;
Heads peering up, peering down
as they have always done,
listening to waves, voices of the heart
that stay with us, move on with us,
play a part in our lives, no matter all
temporal hosts come and gone,
sun and moon out of reach, cabbage
stains on the world's tablecloths...
tales told by shells on Bournemouth
beach of those whose faces may
blur with time but we remember them,
who died of AIDS and not to blame
(the fruits of love bitter-sweet, yet better
by far to live by it than hate)
nor sexuality, physicality, morality,
any match for our own mortality
but as small boats on a passionate sea
driven by a feeling for integrity;
Come a time when death may put love
out of reach, then take a walk
on the sand, talk with the waves, listen
to shells on Bournemouth beach
(or any other that stirs a grieving soul
to recover the heart's grail);
join a passing ship awhile, carrying

Exeter Central Library
Phone enquiries: 0845 155 1001
www.devon.gov.uk/libraries

Borrowed Items 11/09/2013 14:15
XXXXXXXXXX4065

Item Title	Due Date
Accomplices to illusion: pc	02/10/2013
The Ballad of John Henry	18/09/2013

Amount Outstanding : £3.70

You may wish to write the due date on the date label

Local Author Visit Graham Hurley
Wednesday 30th October 7-9 pm
Exeter Central Library

Free drop in sessions
Every Wednesday 10.00 to 12.00
Exeter Central Library

---

family, friends, lovers, even
old neighbours...by day and night,
be they gay or straight...cruise
Loving Memory's fair shores, share
old jokes, laugh about crises
over cabbage stains on best tablecloths

To inner eye (and ear) time never deleted
nor love, though AIDS, ever defeated

[Bournemouth, Dorset, March 2006)

Note:

I have read to audiences in Bournemouth (UK) on several occasions. After one if these, I felt very privileged to be asked by its chairman to write a poem for DAMSET, an HIV-AIDS Awareness project in Dorset. **http://damset.co.uk**

I feel very strongly that there should be more such projects and the world in general is failing its young people by an appalling complacency towards the spread of HIV-AIDS. Far more needs to be done by way of educating adults and children and raising awareness.

DAMSET has involved local schoolchildren in its creating a memorial mural to people in Dorset who have died of AIDS. - *RNT*

·······································

"It is bad enough that people are dying of AIDS , but no one should die of ignorance." – Elizabeth Taylor

"Let us give publicity to HIV/AIDS and not hide it, because the only way to make it appear like a normal illness like TB, like cancer, is always to come out and to say somebody has died because of HIV/AIDS ... And people will stop regarding it as something extraordinary." – Nelson Mandela

·······································

PART 1

ACCOMPLICES TO ILLUSION

ACCOMPLICES TO ILLUSION

Snowflakes, like miniature chandeliers
performing a magic show

Silvery shadows, dancing across fields
like the homeless at a party

North star, a shiny nugget of white gold;
moon slopes like ski runs

Owl, hunting down the ghosts of spring
to what passes for their fate

White Rabbit knows a trick or two, finds
sanctuary in a storybook

Carrot-nose snowman kept busy posing
for Christmas cards

Churches, mosques, synagogues - iced
like birthday cakes

First light of day, Apollo starts throwing
cold water on it all

Party over, the homeless left to work what
magic they can on a world in denial

BACK TO NATURE

I discovered a dirt track in my dreams,
in countryside where the sun always shines,
green acres for miles, as fair as it seems;
no sky trails, no highways, no railway lines

Let me haunt tall forests smelling of spring
in a world where the light of love still shines,
nurture flowers of the heart and we'll sing;
no sky trails, no highways, no railway lines

Have a care, the trees whisper warningly,
though it seem to lovers light always shines
where acid rain may yet kill each daisy,
be sky trails, or highways, or railway lines

Ah, but hear Earth Mother singing sweetly,
"I'm here for you as long as you for me."

A COMMON GARDEN SNAPSHOT

Lives, strewn about in the mud
like underwear torn from a washing line
by a freak wind

Lies, piling up like dead leaves
providing sustenance for the very earth
that nurtured

Hearts, now joined together,
now ripped apart, like bread fought over
by sparrows

Hopes, tossed like underwear
on a cruel wind over hungry graves ready
to gobble us up

Chase the wind, stumble in mud,
retrieve underwear for the washing machine
or stand by and watch?

Choices, a gathering of sparrows
debating how best to survive a bad winter
through to spring

Graves, wearing badges
of flowers and dead leaves, each telling lies
about us

THE BRIDGE

It sings, the bridge at night,
like a hump whale
though softer than by day,
shrouded in mystery
like the fog that descends
now and then...
reminding us that nature
rarely has the ways
of men at heart as we purport
to have its at ours;
Crossing a bay comprising
a magic ages old
in a car's headlights heading
for town, reflections
of moon and stars looking on
at lonely people
peering down, seeking within
for the will to...live?
fighting off persuasive ghosts
(no children at play, these
but stray river genies bent on
mischief or worse)
turning to the bridge for secrets
kept for years in pockets
of love, loss, dreams enough
to make any man, woman,
want to laugh, cry, live...die?

Cars, stars, turning tide of voices;
Bridge of Choices

REDISCOVERING CLIMATE CHANGE

Preserved in ice, like some
prehistoric monster
poised to tread weeping clay,
dead water

Traces of green, shades of envy
to the probing eye
investigating its reappearance
and repercussions

Provoking alarm in Big Brother's
desolate backyard
stretching endlessly, like
a yawning clay pit

Hysteria among humanoid
and robotic camps alike,
tugging at the archaeologist's arm
to leave well alone

Preserved in ice, like some
prehistoric monster;
stirrings of abandoned humanity,
Statue of Liberty

A NATURE LOVER'S DREAM

I've walked live woodlands at night,
heard a nightingale sing, watched
blackbirds to the nest homeward fly,
a shooting star prick an owl's wing,
and trees sweeping stars from the sky;
I've seen rabbits outrun foxes,
badgers outwit baiters (now and then)
moles defy blindness, bats surface,
fireflies dissemble, Man in the Moon
snuggle up to a sleeping swan

I've walked live woodlands at night,
released a hare caught in a trap,
seen poachers retrieve, try to bag more,
harried only by time passing - and
an owl's low, haunting cry. Once, I saw
a fox catch a rabbit, rip it to pieces…
hid and saw badger baiters do their worst
at what they dare to call 'sport' while
even fair Cassiopeia could but sell
Mother Nature short that night

I let live woodlands loose in my head
and they left me for dead

AGENDA FOR A CULL

Seal pups dying,
a culling to complete;
ice caps crying

Bargain prices wing
around the tourist beat;
seal pups dying

Come spring,
craving summer's heat;
ice caps crying

The done thing
to alt-control-delete;
seal pups dying

Greens piling
on the global heat;
ice caps crying

G8 trying
to make ends meet?
seal pups dying,
ice caps crying

THE SQUIRREL

The sun, it shone like a torch among shadows
as we walked misty paths, a friend and I,
observed by a grey squirrel scratching its nose
with its paws, curious perhaps about humans
(why male and female on hind legs, baring claws?)

We parried words in that fast dimming twilight,
guided by the anger in each other's eyes
observed by the grey squirrel scratching its nose
with its paws, curious perhaps about humans
(why, even come eventide, making so much noise?)

Sun and shadows, they surrendered to a frosty night
and stars looked down on us with much the same
curiosity as the squirrel, finished scratching its nose
with its paws, given up caring about humans
(now warring, now hugging or taking other liberties)

Whenever I see a grey squirrel scratching its nose,
I wonder…whatever happened to us?

SPRING IS A GIRL IN A BLUE PRINT DRESS

In a patch of bluebells I met a girl
wearing a blue print dress,
smelling of rain, singing a song
about love, joy and peace;
Laughing, she took me by the hand,
led me a dance as lightly
as a spring breeze teasing leaves,
stroking a dove's feathers,
running exciting fingers
through my hair, making me feel
so…alive

When I asked her name, she smiled
and burst into song again
without answering, lifting my heart
like the dove's wing,
parading a glowing pregnancy
at heaven's battered gate
as if half expecting to be kept out
for reshaping a wintry world,
holding God to His word,
demonstrating a capacity for peace,
keeping hope…alive

A heavy shower broke. We took up
an offer of shelter
from a friendly tree, leaves of green
already playing host
to assorted couples, some foreign,
but when I turned, that girl
in a pretty blue print dress was gone;
I searched long and hard till
soaked to the skin before
escaping a predatory sadness inside,
nearly…died

For sun and showers, joy or distress,
spring wears a blue print dress for us

SUMMER IS A MAN IN A BLUE DENIM SHIRT

In a field of sunflowers I met a man
wearing a blue denim shirt,
smelling of roses, singing a song
about love, joy and peace;
Laughing, he took me by the hand,
led me a dance as lightly
as a summer wind's teasing leaves,
stroking a sparrow's feathers,
running friendly fingers
through my hair, making me feel
so…alive

When I asked his name, he smiled
and burst into song again
without answering, lifting my heart
like the sparrow's wing,
flirting with clouds at heaven's door
as if daring someone to fling
it wide and protest at such blasphemy
as behaving so badly we even
whisper gossip at prayers
intended to give thanks for being
so…alive

A dark storm broke. We could but run
for the shelter and safety
of a nearby farmhouse painted green
but when I turned, that man
in the faded blue denim shirt was gone;
I searched long and hard
in pouring rain until soaked to the skin
before finally knocking at the door,
no sign of life so had to move on,
nearly…died

Come sun or storms, see summer pass,
its heart left waiting on love and peace

AUTUMN IS A MAN IN RED

In a garden spread with dead leaves
and heads of flowers,
I heard a story told by a dying rose
about to breathe its last,
about a Man in Red passing through
the world scaring us
like the Bogey Man who lives under
a child's bed, pretending to roar
like a dragon out for sport
yet made to look small, caught out
like the family pet

Neither young nor old, the Man in Red
wears buttons of gold
on a coat the colour of blushing cheeks
at our making a faux pas,
made to look as small as a dragon under
our bed at night long ago
when every dawn a prologue to adventure
though, by sunset, traces of blood
enough to make us glad
computer games are but fairytale
gone mad

According to the rose, this Man in Red
has kindly ways
in spite of luring savage cloud and wind
like hungry beasts
to feed off gentle trees, rip them bare
while a few songbirds dare
watch and wonder about songs they once
made, turned into dreams then
gave a friendly sandman
to paint the world's bleakest scenarios
with brave colours

He comes for me, said the rose, and I depart
though the Man in Red keep me in his heart

WINTER IS A WOMAN IN WHITE

Where once daisies in meadows green
footmarks where Jack Frost
has paused, glanced over his shoulder
for any sign
of a Woman in White haunting each step
he takes…
marking each heavy, careless tread,
all green things left for dead
that may yet be saved
to bring life and glory to another season
under her protection

She'll bide her time before descending
on wings of a dove
that spreads its wings like an eiderdown
of white satin
where a restless world dreams of waking
to a peace and goodwill
folk singers will sing for years,
church choirs berate
near empty pews,
world leaders slip into election speeches
and Sunday prayers

She'll not stay long, though time well spent
making good at least
some of the damage old Jack inclined to do,
reminding poor robin,
its tears almost done, of other garden lives
sleeping off hangovers
from half forgotten centuries lusting
for the joys of spring,
lost in the making
of wars on nature's own, more careless even
and deadlier than Jack's

As peace to its sacrifices, so glory to the pain
of the Woman in White, once come and gone

LINES ON NATURE CONSERVATION

'Death'
such a sad, lonely word,
flies above us like a graceful bird
but makes no sound
nor will it ever descend to breathe
life and love into a tree
or flex its wings on our window sill;
we can but watch, learn, dare
to flex our own, breathe
life and love into a tree, no matter
where it be, for there I will
sit with you and you will sit with me,
watching a bird on wing
bring grace to the greyest skies
nor any fairer sound
till joined by another then hear both
sing loud and clear, a poem
for the trees to share night and day
long, long after we have
gone away

POND LIFE

Lily pads, sharing
love's secrets

Sunlight, drawing
on its magic

Swans, smoothing
ruffled feathers

Blue sky, shedding
portent clouds

Ripples, rewriting
old love poems

Lily pads, opening
up our hearts

A WALK IN BLEAN WOODS

Blean Woods, leaves shades of gold,
memories, like swallows, seeking kinder days,
bonfire of our vanities never grown cold

Domesday tales by the same trees told,
painting a pretty picture come sunlight's haze;
Blean Woods, leaves shades of gold

Autumn passes, leaves gone for mould,
kaleidoscope turns on winter's whimsical ways;
bonfire of our vanities never grown cold

Sweet music in leafy skies, let spring unfold,
go with peace to that place where it seldom stays;
Blean Woods, leaves shades of gold

Too few pause to hear, listen, learn, behold
till only cock robin's left to sing beauty's praise;
bonfire of our vanities never grown cold

Time passes. In tears, the same tales told;
Armageddon, a bleak picture come sunlight's haze;
Blean Woods, leaves shades of gold,
bonfire of our vanities never grown cold

[Canterbury, Nov.11th 2006]

IN THE COMPANY OF DOLPHINS
(For Friends & Lovers Everywhere)

I think of us at twilight's gentler tears
on flowers in a pretty garden, glistening
like ocean spray in spring sunshine;
In the mind's eye, I see survivors
clinging to the wreckage of a ship that
safe harbours will never greet again…
and dolphins come like guardian angels
to redeem a fate demanded by storm clouds
riding old Poseidon's back

Now calmer seas, survivors washed up
on kinder shores, dolphins gone, task done;
Lost souls saved at godly whim?
I know not, can but let heart and mind
wish the company of dolphins to bring us
safely home…and though that be left
to this sad world's darker poetry,
may love's light shine through twilight's
gentler tears on us

A FEELING FOR SEAGULLS
(For Everyone at OUTCOME)

Coming together, supporting each other,
toes in the Sea of Life, getting a feel for the swim
rather than drown

Making an effort to come down to a shore
with seaweed and shells on shifting sands spread
rather than stay in bed

A part of the tide's natural ebb and flow
yet frightened of a fickle nature, its highs and lows
but a Hall of Mirrors

Alone, it is hard to bear the happy sounds
of seagulls shrieking, applause for ice cream chimes,
hints at kinder times

In good company, easier by far to break free
of shadows stalking us, driving us to seek sanctuary
in cages of our history

Together, let's imagine wings, flex and fly,
take heart from gulls rejoicing our seas, shores, sky…
no matter where or why

As rough or fair as any sea passage may be,
let us look to fellow voyagers, let a creative empathy
reconstruct our history

Coming together, supporting each other,
getting a feel for wings rising above, learning how
to trust in Nature's love

THE HORSE WHISPERER

Foaming passions crashing down
on this, my art

God's stallions on a last ditch run
of poetry…

Apollo, master-catcher, anxious
to break us in

Ghosts in the frame calling us out
in heaven's name

Salty tears, a sandman's labours
all but won

Lead palomino rears, cries, bows,
spirit unbroken

Leaning forward to bend its ear,
I, the horse whisperer

ETERNITY REVISITED
(For Stuart M.)

See purple peaks, draped in mist,
enchanting a lowlander's eye;
Cumbrian fells, by heaven kissed

A storm cloud, like a devil's fist
bringing down a passive sky;
see purple peaks, draped in mist

Paths of glory discovered, missed;
defenders of faiths, loath to die;
Cumbrian fells, by heaven kissed

Here, an age and beauty co-exist
that pass Man's inhumanity by;
see purple peaks, draped in mist

Let walkers, climbers, lovers tryst
and lakes all Nature let fly;
Cumbrian fells, by heaven kissed

Where history its myths can't resist
and old gods may laugh or cry,
see purple peaks, draped in mist,
Cumbrian fells, by heaven kissed

[Carlisle, Cumbria, June 2006]

A FEELING FOR SPRING

Clouds, like soft soap bubbles giving
shape to wet dreams

Birds, but pretty spots on tired eyes,
a cacophony on the ear

Trees, like the bony legs of old men
standing firm

Leaves, like prayer beads in the hands
of a dying nun

Grass, a doormat enduring the heavy
tread of world competition

Earth, but a sheet of clay, camouflage
for centuries of ambition

Ah, but a fair butterfly, fair phoenix
flying in the face of despair…

Grasshoppers, raising a rousing hymn
to Mother Nature

She, smiling like the nun through pain,
senses alive to spring

Daffodils, cheering us all on, no matter
if we win or lose

Heaven, though butt of the world's flaws,
throwing open its doors

SWAN LAKE

A love story on stage;
nerve strings of its composer
turning each page

As a bird flies its cage,
so music in glorious colour;
a love story on stage

Let dance, our pain assuage;
ensemble, solo, or pas de deux
turning each page

See art display the courage
of humankind's old enemy, fear;
a love story on stage

Performance, paying homage
to the divided heart of its creator,
turning each page

Dancers, their talents engage
to read into art all human nature;
a love story on stage
turning each page

[Harlow, Essex, April 2007]

Note: Written after a performance by the Harlow
Ballet Association at the Playhouse, Harlow.

BEATING UP THE PLANET

Running a gamut of earthquakes,
beating the flames

Sheltering in Iraq from bullets
beating down

Watching children of a lesser god
beating up butterflies

Letting our leaders get away with
beating drums

Standing for democracy's bouncers
beating up flowers

Paying a price for politic players
beating the odds

Treating poverty's weeping wounds,
(beating its hunger?)

Singing praises to a Greater Power,
(beating terror?)

Preparing to swim with polar bears,
beating ourselves up

REAR WINDOW

Daylight's rear window,
weeping gashes,
knives in the back,
history revisited

Impatient stars pricking
their way through
the carbon, dotting i's
and crossing t's

On a lawn below, daisy
patches like graves for
brave words, home truths
left in the air

Sun gone, no encryption
left on the window,
only ghosts knocking
to be let in

Bitter-sweet end, a match
even for that mystique
some call a soul, others
conscience

PART 2
WHATEVER HAPPENED TO LOVE?

WHATEVER HAPPENED TO LOVE?

Peace in the park abused by druggies
desperate to fund the luxury;
No time for drugs? Lets go for alcohol
poisoning instead…

Fun at the fair ruined by pickpockets
out for an easy ride;
Sanctuary in our schools invaded
by a culture of bullying

Generation gaps made (far) wider
by five star psychiatrists;
Mother Nature repeatedly raped
by property developers

War on Terror, a welcome distraction
from Home Front issues;
Our own back yards piled high
with body bags…

Conscience part salved by more charity,
confession, prison programs…
Problem part solved by pointing fingers
of blame elsewhere

Facts of life, we're told and no point
in crying over spilt blood;
Prevention better than cure, they say,
so whatever happened to love?

BONDING WITH ETERNITY
(For Joyce & Charles)

It was love opened up my heart
to all life means to me...
nor shall death its bonding part

Sands of time, soulmates at the start,
a song of destiny;
it was love opened up my heart

May the world no finer truths impart
than its natural beauty;
nor shall death its bonding part

Like summer skies, stars, even clouds
charting a fragile humanity...
it was love opened up my heart

If a taste on the tongue sweet or tart,
our togetherness a delicacy;
nor shall death its bonding part

Be nature's kin struck by a poison dart
comprising all inhumanity...
it was love opened up my heart
nor shall death its bonding part

LOVE ENDURES

It was midwinter, but in your arms,
a summer's heat…
on your lips, a taste of spring

Snow flurries kindly wrapped us up
in cotton wool…
hid us from cruel prejudices

Spring came, its songs of love and joy
in our hearts…
outing us to family and friends

Come summer, we'd run hand in hand
this gauntlet and that…
of sneers, jeers, crass remarks

By autumn, we were sick of persistently
being dumped…
on piles of red, dead leaves

Next midwinter, we moved in together,
gave a party…
and those who came were glad for us

Seasons come and go, but in your arms
a summer's heat…
on your lips, a taste of spring

ONE DAY

One day to remember, one day to forget;
One day bringing us together, another
tearing us apart

One day for friendship, one day for rage;
One day for love, another
blotting its page

One day to be sure, another to doubt;
One day in your bed, another
in a rush to get out

One day peace, one day panic alarms;
One day heat and joy, another
grown old in your arms

One day, life's lessons to learn and share;
One day bringing us together, another
finding us still there

THE ROSE LOVER

Coveting a first spring rose,
I saw petals break away, chase
each other like star-crossed
lovers in a play, harried high
and low, nature's way;
Now, seized by a gust (needs
must as the devil drives);
Now, lulled by kinder tongues
to a daisy patch. Alas,
no match for race horse hooves
chasing after a butterfly;
Continuing to covet, tired eyes
half-closed against the sun,
I am trampled along with those
petals in the grass. Neither
nature's gain or loss, this death
of a lonely rose lover, save
hoof prints on the heart where
you gave chase to a butterfly
(prettier than I) and even now
fresh daisies mark my grave

WEATHERING LOVE

When I dream of you, it is a springtime
of high hopes I'll not forget

When I think of you, it is midsummer,
(that rainy day we first met)

When I speak of you, each word is like
an autumn leaf that's falling

When I hear your name on another's lips
it's but a winter robin calling

At nature's whims, a beauty, each its own
though we weather it alone…

THE ZEN OF FLOWER ARRANGING

Flowers in my window because I love you;
Flowers in my window to show how I care;
Flowers in my window, still dreaming of you;
Flowers in my window to tell you I'm near

Flowers in my window, story of our love,
a sweet dream of springtime in winter's sigh;
Flowers in my window, such treasures to give,
as we gave to each other, you and I

Flowers in my window, reflections of you;
Flowers in my window, highlights in your hair;
Flowers in my window because love runs true;
Flowers in my window remind me you're near

Dreams in my window, we'll always believe;
Dreams in my window, you left on your grave

NO HANDOUTS

Love, given freely, expects nothing,
though love returned is a beautiful thing;
yet love asks and deserves respect, nor
should endure less, even for its own sake;
For loved ones, yes, we do our best
by a heart's palpitations, yet if its returns
measure less, dare we bury our deeper
frustrations, let darker corners of the mind
become a makeshift tomb?

I love someone and love him dearly
(knowing full well he does not love me)
take our being together at face value,
sense no conflict on his part allowing for
any hurt he'll cause me, pain inflicted
on my heart. That he calls me 'mate' but
safe-distances me, acknowledges us
close friends, permits our intimacy to pass
for a sense of spirituality

He treats my love with contempt
(over and over again) though I suspect
he has never so much as glimpsed
the scars on my soul, this man without
vision to see, imagination to grasp
how love, in all its shapes, combinations,
is as fragile as it is strong…like smoke
rings from a cigar, patches on a one legged
street beggar's sleeve.

Though sun, moon, stars, write its poems,
no such handouts for love's victims

SEPARATE STONES

One summer we lay beneath a willow tree,
gazing at a fluffy, leafy, sky,
passionate branches like arms around me,
enduring river flowing idly by

Time then to laugh, play, see kingfishers dive
for shimmering scales defying capture
in vain, an inspired will to stay alive
to the last breath, like love's gasping rapture

Daring to dream, we made that summer ours,
let joyful birdsong drown the river's sighs
till autumn's beating at heaven's towers
brought us, half-listening, to the world's lies

Though some mourn, scorn stones separating us,
let the willow weep for them, not our ghosts

SECRET LOVE

For you alone my soul on view,
its prayer no God dare let come true;
in death, too, grieved most by you

My heart, our dream, it tore in two
though any who chanced to see but few;
for you alone, my soul on view

Hope, it was, that saw me through,
each twilight's bitter-sweet kiss renew;
in death, too, grieved most by you

Though little I had, like a tree it grew,
autumn leaves among skies spring blue;
for you alone, my soul on view

To my secret love, I stayed true,
far richer for the poorer life through;
in death, too, grieved most by you

Inspiration from your smile I drew;
on sunset's lips our every lie rang true;
For you alone my soul on view;
in death, too, grieved most by you

RUMMAGING THE ARCHIVES
(For Malcolm H)

Home truths, like near dead lilies on a lake
running dry

Lifelines, like veins of a turning leaf
come autumn

Desire, taking comfort in homemade soup
in winter

Wisdom, taking its cue from the first
cuckoo of spring

Ambition, but Jack Frost's tablecloth spread,
our places laid

Passion, saving water lilies from a lake
running dry

Love, preserving archives lest humanity
need reminding what it is

NIGHT WATCH

I have greeted chimes at midnight,
lain half dead at the toll for one
as my lifeblood ebbs to a starlight
behind clouds, watch all but done

I have heard the clock ticking over,
for the passing of happy hours…
nor shall, when it stops, run for cover
but embrace a time forever ours

I have heard sweet songs at sunrise,
watched the last stars slip away,
seen my life's light in your bright eyes
promise a beautiful spring day

As nature pauses at stark winter's cold,
so lovers dream, beyond a growing old

TOO LATE FOR POETRY

As I lay on a pillow thinking of us,
he opened the door and came in,
crossed to the bed, lay down beside me,
cradled my head, swore he loved me,
would see me through my agony
(knowing you'd cheated on me again)
begging to share a bed left as sad
and lonely as that shroud in which our
love left to lie, letting fly a desire
to write the final page of a dark history
that had seen you and I feed off our
need for each other, making believe we
were in love and nothing else should
matter (even lies, deception) only a risen
to heaven on wings of sex and desire
though flames of hellfire lick at the soles
of our feet, eager to devour us once
our fair flight done and we fallen angels
tumble into a pit no phoenix dare risk
unless (the stranger whispers in my ear)
we quit soap opera, aspire to the poetry
of truth, hope, even glory

A tempting offer! Almost fooled by tears
then suddenly saw through the disguise,
told you straight…enough lies; nor was it
God's way of punishing us, we'd already
seen to that ourselves

COVENANT WITH LOVE

Though saddened hearts would break
and HIV-AIDS a rising toll,
love, with loss, its peace shall make

Watch ripples spread on heaven's lake,
sun and moon, fair heart and soul,
though saddened hearts would break

Come disease, fate, or God lives take,
anger, grief, like burning coal,
love, with loss, its peace shall make

See a light from dark, its prison break,
let better times roll…
though saddened hearts would break

Though we live for living's own sake,
no matter affairs of the soul,
love, with loss, its peace shall make

Let the world's worst its own forsake
and healing be our goal;
though saddened hearts would break,
love, with loss, its peace shall make

OPEN WINDOW

Though ears never hear a word spoken
or life's everyday sounds at the door,
there's a window be sure to leave open
for love's spirit that seeks to reassure

It reads your lips, hears all you have to say
that I might not understand when you sign;
if lips and hands gone silent, as they may,
let love's spirit run free, our thoughts divine

We may quarrel, as hearing people do
and making up will be its own reward,
love's spirit telling us what we should do,
knowing we will hear its every word

The spirit of love speaks to mind and heart;
deaf or hearing, we can but play our part

SUNNY DAYS, PASSING STORMS

There is a winter sunshine breaking
through a fine mist of fun things done,
sunnier places known, kinder times,
to memory consigned yet retrieved now
and then and gladly, especially when
we are lonely, to enjoy again like a toy
kept in a special place that's yours,
mine, ours, for rediscovering the things
that matter more than tears of self-pity,
like the simple joys and a peace of mind
kept safe by friendship's hugs, kisses,
cuddles, confiding poems, making plans
(though they be daydreams) – each
caring about the other, even when apart,
and if fiction against fact should ever
conspire to distract us and a storm break,
we can weather whatever human nature
conjures up for us

No friendship more sure than on itself
freely feeding, its love enduring, no
matter that some seize any opportunity
to malign, redefine its intimacy

AT FREEDOM'S CALL

Once I played in green hills at high summer,
listening to birds sing, watching them fly,
ran free, hand in hand with my gay lover
our dream, like a kite, reaching for the sky

In purple hills, come autumn's reds and gold,
I watched birds winging free of winter's threat,
leaves painting pictures of we two grown old,
our dream, like a kite, playing hard to get

Once I walked in white hills at winter's call,
heard a robin sing in branches stripped bare,
nor did it take flight at the first snowfall,
our dream, like a kite, sure to please me there

If summer short, autumn brief, winter dead,
be love's eternal spring taken as read

MISTY MEMORIES
(For Auntie Bridie)

Let love be painting pictures on the heart
for the soul's grasp forever to retain,
so the mind's eye, less clear than at the start
and peering though mist, may enjoy again

Though memory's jigsaw may fall apart,
fitting its pieces, we make wrong choices,
the mind's ear, if less clear than at the start
is still listening out, hears love's voices

Our finer senses, heart and soul shall hone,
if seen to work in mysterious ways,
so Memory, though fair stripped to the bone,
to the inner self stay true all our days

Though love but shadows in a timeless mist,
take heart, all whom its poetry has kissed

BEAUTY AND THE BEAST

Be lust on love left to feast
since time began,
it is Beauty kills the Beast

Desire, it but lasts the least
in woman or man,
be lust on love left to feast

Though a devil play priest
as well it can,
it is Beauty kills the Beast

Come dark silences in tryst
to the grave of Pan,
be lust on love left to feast

A rogue sandman deceased,
shot down as he ran;
it is Beauty kills the Beast

Faith in humanity increased
by one Good Samaritan;
Be lust on love left to feast,
it is Beauty kills the Beast

LAST CALL

Last crabs on the beach,
last clouds dispersing;
last sea spray in the hair,
last gull seen diving;
Last waves touching toes,
last ice cream chimes,
last view from the tower,
last trip on tramlines;
Last giggle at postcards,
last cuppa in our café,
last stroll on South pier,
last of a summer's day;
Last dash for the station,
last train, just in time…
last carriage, getting use
to being on my own

Last thought, eyes closing,
of our lips kissing;
Last wish, heart pounding,
a love everlasting

Last text message, reading
between the lines;
Last call, a first love poem
to remember us by

[Blackpool, Lancs., 2000]

MAKING UP FOR WINTER

We sat on a bench looking out at the sea;
you edged closer, laid a hand on my knee,
arms around each other the way friends do
only this time, something different, new

I felt your hand move until it found mine,
caress my fingers lightly then entwine;
hot breath on my cheek like intimate lace
though I dare not turn, look you in the face

Not a word, your head on my shoulder,
my mind in turmoil, heart beating louder;
I froze and hastily you pulled away,
winter closing in on us, sad and grey

I turned, licked my lips and leapt the abyss;
on the other side, we shared our first kiss

POLITICS OF THE HEART

Some jeered when you came out
and told the world you're gay;
to my great shame, I took their part
let ignorance win the day

For weeks, I implored my alter ego
to rise above a pillow's tears,
let me shout how I have loved you
though hid behind my fears

Some were scornful when I came out
and told the world I'm gay;
to my surprise and pride, I cared not,
only that truth had won the day

It was a while before I dared face you,
confess the hypocrite I'd been,
how I longed to hold and kiss you,
held back 'cause taught obscene

Your heart but took its cue from mine
and rushed straight in…
to dry my tears with spring sunshine,
absolve them with its passion

Some still jeer at a love much derided,
harsh words spoken…
the world's churches openly divided
on blessing gay men and women

Scarier still, the rogue heart's ambition
to be applauded casting that first stone

PINK IN THE FRAME

Yellow, like bright sunshine on spring flowers;
such is the colour of love

Green, like summer leaves dancing on a breeze;
such is the colour of love

Sometimes turning a reddish gold, growing old;
such is the colour of love

Sometimes gone grey, like our ashes in a hearth;
such is the colour of love

White, like virgin snow on nature's fine promises;
such is the colour of love

Pink, like dawn's gay chorus or sunset's shy blush;
such, too, is the colour of love

SHIFTING THE BURDEN

In the rain, an acid rain, you're there
lifting the burden of my despair

Let the world roll out another century,
consigning us to memory,
clouds forbid the sun and heaven weep;
in my dark, your light I'll keep
till this mere flesh no more can stand
and Death lends us a hand
as through a graveyard in acid rain
we will walk and talk again

In the rain, an acid rain, you're there,
lifting the burden of my despair

Though the world, it blast into infinity,
consigning us to the galaxy,
yet seedlings shall survive, endure
in Mother Nature's loving care
till a semblance of Eden form yet again
the killing fields of God and Man
and through graveyards in acid rain
they will walk and talk again

In the rain, an acid rain, we're here
lifting the burden of their despair

CURTAIN RISING
(For Liam R.)

Heart feeling top-heavy, an
ache in the soul;
no one here to listen,
everyone on vacation – or
an answering machine?
Time to try again - say
life's worthwhile,
see sunshine through rain
making pretty flowers grow,
a heaven in the know
wiping tears, putting a smile
on faces lined with pain
for going that last lonely mile
with friends who let us down,
loved ones dead and gone

Listen! For birds singing - in
this field, that city or town;
Look for children playing, lovers
wishing on stars, a good earth
enduring, for all its tears

Troubled mind, a summer mist;
in its curtain rising, let us trust

PART 3

DIRTY DANCING

PRIVATE LIVES

Scraps of a letter left floating down a gutter
nudging a pretend-impassive shoreline

People drifting past, half an eye on blue ink
stains, wondering to whom, by, even why?

It doesn't matter of course, mere history now,
despatched to the nearest drain

Yet someone had once made the time to think,
feel, write, read, decide to throw away

Secrets passing between two people found out
and punished, disowned…or forgiven?

Lovers, friends, family…left on opposite sides
of some religious divide?

Who discovered, betrayed, turned fine feelings
into a blur of anonymous ink stains?

In a heat now, over scraps of a letter last seen
sucking the life out someone's history

Memories revived, quickly mowed down by rolls
of thunder, anxious to leave no trace

More rain, gutter a river, scraps gone to sewage
under a city smelling of secrets

DIRTY DANCING

I can be friend or foe, take me as you will
into a corner of your heart and let me stay
to whisper sweet words of love and desire
in your ear, bring precious respite from life's
bitter trials, wars and sleepless nights…
for worry, fear, a dread of what the dawn
may devour. I'll be a light in your darkness
if you care, or else we dare to dance
the shadow-line, win or lose

I can be friend or foe, take me as you will
into a corner of your soul and let me stay
to whisper cruel words of lust and desire
in your ear, though no respite from life's
bitter trials, wars and sleepless nights…
for worry, fear, a dread of what the dawn
may devour. What's this? Let darkness fall
upon all we have conspired with a love
of money, to prove ourselves?

No! See these parts that comprise a whole
that can be taken for friend or foe, as you
will, and take from me all you need to fire
the heart, ease the soul…for good or ill,
young or old, though all that glisters
is not gold nor dreamers fools who love
and live every day as if their last, but see
in me distortions of our better selves
that faithless shadows cast

Though you find me out on the shadow-line,
dare give the dance a name, call it ambition

GOING FOR BROKE

No prejudices, but engaging in
political correctness among the rich,
poor, deaf, hearing, blind, mute,
wheelchair-bound or dead keen on
fun runs for this or that charity
set up by agreeing to act in absentia
for the world's conscience, broking
failures to conform to what its betters
have identified as 'norm'

Foil for a deaf priest in Soweto,
a housewife doing battle with cancer
on a bicycle; rock stars in Africa;
cause to pause, consider participating
in love's healing light that's here
for the seeking, taking, letting grow
the most beautiful flower, no mind
its kinder soil gone for another office
block, motorway or landfill

Music, dance, poetry…putting
questions we dare not ask ourselves;
paintings, sculptures, expressing
centuries of need, desire, whatever
we choose to make of a fire raging
within, supplying that heat and light
we might care to attribute to a soul
and reminding us we all have a share
should we but care to play fair

While never easy to put one over on me,
some do, though I am called Adversity

NO STRATEGY FOR SURRENDER

Cliffs, like dark angels attacking from the sea
only to hover defiantly between a misty
earth and sky, like bats in glass cages, choice
specimens to admire, touch even, without
fear (or real appreciation). Nor are we safe, for
they dare fly in our faces like the worst vices
intimidating us, blindly excusing themselves,
arousing a native curiosity no matter how hard
we try to keep our distance. Now, all is quiet.
Now, a rush of wings depriving our eyes of light
and other sounds at ears listening out for cries
of warning, reassurance (what else?) luring us
to nether regions of a soul inciting us to view
dark angels with awe for daring to exhibit, expose,
our shortcomings. We can but watch, linger...
afraid and suitably repressed by (whose?) criteria
for a civilized life that brooks little empathy
with dark angels deemed to have made bad choices,
excluded for flying with bats (safety in numbers?)
frozen in a frantic rhythm imposed by heaven,
composed by poets, lusted after by self-styled
adventurers; natural sensibility vying with human
accountability, sun's glare with shadows summoned
from the Black Hole of a maturity eroded by time,
only to be pitted against an omnipresence for a place
in its history before resistance made to crumble,
last seen beating a retreat to Poseidon's lair, nor any
hope or sanctuary there, old gods long since deposited
in ghost cathedrals and left wringing their hands

OBSESSION

I'll make a hunchback of you,
both feet gripping the waist,
teeth in the neck aborting
every true word you try to say
though you do not comprehend
the fix you're in, vaguely aware
of some discomfort but unable
(unwilling) to track its source
but carry on regardless

I'll make a fool of you, object
of scorn (though tempered
with compassion among family
and friends who dare not say so
or you'll be certain to interpret it
as interference at best, pity
at worst). Oblivious to passion's
blind spot, you embrace me
in your heart

I'll make a loser out of you, unless
you choose to take me on, recognize
the enemy within for what I am
or else go as a lamb to the slaughter
at the altar of alter ego, seeking
shelter from life's storms in love's
inviting harbours - but as a guest,
no sense of belonging, only
a hungry yearning

Bold, the hunchback who escapes me,
at Desire's kinder side goes free

FAT UNDER FIRE
(For Angie & Dan)

Lumbering down a High Street
with the shopping, well aware
of folks gawking, passing comment
along lines of denying fat people
the same equal rights as the rest of us
to push and shove, stop and chat,
others trying to pass and not looking
where we're going anyway, too
busy on the mobile phoning to say
we'll be late, delayed by a fatty
in front of us, no thought for other
people's priorities.

No room on the bus to spread out
on a seat, the person next to us
too fat for words; as for cramming
a tube train, have fatties no shame?

Mugged yesterday, sent sprawling,
crowd stepping over me, probably
thinking I'm just another drunk, druggie
or nuisance homeless, mouth dribbling,
senses unable to pull together until
later thanking a fat couple who stopped,
helped, flagged down a cab to take me
home at their own expense

Note: An earlier version of this poem was published
in *Shaft Of Light*, Poetry Now, 2003.

OPEN ROAD
(For Amy A.)

Found myself one day
on a road I did not know;
kept walking anyway,
no place else to go

Past fields once green,
houses an ugly, silent grey;
landscape obscene,
ash on the clay

Bend after bend, afraid
of all I knew I'd surely find,
down to land mines laid
of the political kind

Sick of unholy collusion
contrived daily for His glory
(no matter our religion)
God, but history

So, no sign of salvation
or even a lifeline in prayer;
any hope of redemption
reduced to metaphor

Suddenly, I began to see
as if in a fog starting to clear,
it wasn't the road but me
going nowhere

Woken from a nightmare,
I was just in time to discover
Apollo tugging at one ear,
a fool at the other

Sunlight, an open road,
from bedlam took me away
as I walked unafraid
into a new day

COMING, READY OR NOT

Once, but a child, tugging at a mother's
apron strings

Once, bunking off school, scared
of bullies

Once, fell in love but there was no love
in it

Once, more than ambitious enough
to fail

Once, holding back tears at ma's funeral
until years later

Once, filled with nothing but regret
for time misspent

Wiser now, but a V-sign from the ferryman
says 'Coming, ready or not'

REGRET

I move without favour or prejudice
among men, women, children;
To whomsoever calls me out, I will
always answer, no one denied
the music I bring, Blues I sing;
Rich, poor, famous, infamous, saints
and sinners…welcome to tap into
a wisdom some say down to Fate,
lessons learned too late

I touch without favour or prejudice
the loose thread missing a button,
that odd sock, empty vase in rooms
yawning with boredom for what's
on TV and must have heard that CD
a thousand times (surely?) though
any sound better than none and
(finally) settling for a plaintive purr
by a lap tray set for one

I bury without favour or prejudice
forgotten dreams, misspent ideals,
wishful thinking on falling stars…
meant to light a kinder, better world;
alas, not meant to be though we
mull over old letters, photos, poems,
home videos…as dead as the cat
whose meows we miss and listen for
at every mealtime

I move without favour or prejudices
among life's pleasures and losses

THE RHETORIC OF MORTALITY

If I should close my eyes come eventide,
never to see the dawn, who will
think of me as the sun rises on a new day
and I not there to praise?

If I should close my eyes come eventide,
never to hear the dawn, who will
think of me as heaven makes glad music
and I not there to praise?

If I should close my eyes come eventide,
never to smell the dawn, who will
think of me as flowers open their petals
and I not there to praise?

If I should close my eyes come eventide,
never to taste the dawn, who will
think of me as young ones suck the breast
and I not there to praise?

If I should close my eyes come eventide,
never to touch the dawn, who will
think of me, opening windows on the world
and I not there to praise?

If I should close my eyes come eventide,
all but one dream ebb away...
think of me and for life's everyday poetry,
on my behalf, give praise

SPOILT FOR CHOICE

Too often have I talked with Death
in green fields, by sandy shores,
under stars in the middle of the night,
on street corners in broad daylight;
Conversation is always much the same,
along the lines of my losing a grip
on the meaningfulness of life and love
and He offering safety, security,
release from the anxieties of integrity;
Let Death take responsibility for me
where others refuse, be a ghost among
shades of darkness, distanced from
the spoils and heartache of daily grind,
out of sight, out of mind?

Too often have I talked with Death
during early hours, late strolls,
counting spring lambs frolicking in
fields of memory, listening out for
voices across the sea, once near, dear
to me, not so long ago it seems,
stuff of sweet dreams, laid low come
cold light of day, buried beneath
cracked paving stones, cruel highways
expecting me to carry on till I drop
exhausted, reaching for Death's hand
rather than dare ask for help, seek
answers in prayers that always seem
to fall on deaf ears…

"No one cares," Death delights in
telling me, urging that I turn
my back on spite, hate, jealousy,
poverty, hunger, war, a politics
of perversity, world religions busy
practising world division, quick
to condemn what (too often) they
can't comprehend for refusing
to play a part in common workings
of the heart, keeping their distance,
awarding marks out of ten to any seen
to have stakes in a God they would
claim for their own and give a name
where no need for one

Where voices would deny us peace,
let us explore the politics of choice

THE VOICE

I heard a voice singing,
wondered whose it might be?
(I could not see)

I heard a voice laughing,
wondered whose it might be?
(I could not see)

I heard a voice crying,
wondered whose it might be?
(I could not see)

I heard a voice praying,
wondered what (if anything)
to do with me?

I heard the voice dying,
wondered where it might go?
One day I'll know

TESTAMENT TO LIFE

I once kissed death on the cheek as it slept,
let a flow of memories course my veins
while hope past a grieving heart gently crept,
ghost rider tugging gently at the reins

I once kissed death on the lips as it rested
where nature's meaningful tides turn no more
nor its finer spirit's growth arrested
but songs of love and peace, no talk of war

I took death by the hand as it would leave;
its firm, kind, touch wiping away a tear,
prising my fingers gently from its sleeve
in the shade of time's makeshift watchtower

We can but wonder where it is death goes,
and in its wake be sure to plant flowers

A VIEW FROM THE EDGE

On the edge, where I stand,
see lambs alongside lions roam
no man's land

In the ears, a gospel band
playing Pilgrims of Peace home
on the edge, where I stand

By a sleight of nature's hand
as of cleaning rust from chrome;
no man's land

Come twilight, shores of sand,
skies rolling like high seas foam
on the edge, where I stand

Let love, nature withstand,
spring lambs among lions roam
no man's land

Be a world leader's smile bland,
see it deny time's pilgrims a home;
On the edge, where I stand,
no man's land

SIGNING UP WITH AHAB

See green-eyed gods rearing
in the mind's eye,
Ahab in the White House
paying lip service

Policy pundits barking mad
at being ignored
but…a good night at the dogs
(aren't we all vulnerable?)

Body bags shouting the odds
at God's bankers privy
to insider information, buying
precious time

Vainglory, all but done with
chasing its own tail;
Ishmael, kept busy rewriting
the story of a whale

CONTRACT FOR LIFE

I care not for the world as it is now,
yet am told it is because I grow old
and memory paints a prettier picture
of the way things were then, when
the world (and I) were young, songs
about peace by country singers sung
before tinsel pop stars came along
to make good failing sales, playing
the public good at its own game;
feed the world, profile the poor - for
a mere few quid a prayer

I care not for the world as it is now,
yet am told it is because I grow old
and memory plays tricks on a mind,
rummaging the recesses of protest
marches against wars, nuclear stores,
a failure of immigration to tackle
problems integration's sure to bring
(resentment, pain, fear) to everyone
living here, in an island kingdom
said to be united even by those who
see us as we are - divided

I care not for the world as it is now,
yet am told it is because I grow old,
refuse to accept a process of change
in which I can play a part or fall
behind, the choice is mine. Progress
demands we move with new times,
new cultures, no matter arms vultures
promoting a War on Terror, making
the most of what's worst in us,

feeding half lies to wannabe martyrs
seeking a get-out clause

Hieroglyphics in clay and stars,
no get-out clause

IN THE BLINK OF AN EYE

Face of a dead person hints at
a smile

Butterfly spends its last seconds
In flight

TIME SPENT IN A VALLEY

Once I played in a place full of shadows,
chasing after them as I might butterflies,
trying to catch but always failing, dropping
to the ground in fits of laughter rippling
across a valley like raindrops on that lake
where I'd swim among ducks and swans
in hues of silver, gold, pink, come the sun's
yawning at dawn, glaring at noon, roaming
Memory Lane in a twilight spitting blood at
sunsets reminiscent of this world's wars
whose shadows, to its own design, always
find a source to blame, scapegoat to ease
the consciences of poor souls born to front
a politics of separatism

Years on, I revisited those same shadows,
wary of them as I might be of ghosts,
trying to hide but always failing, cowering
in corners praying to a Heaven I doubted
that I'd not be discovered or, if so, not taken
in shackles to some cliff edge and forced
to contemplate awful lies told, mistakes made,
excuses given for believing in justification
(or glorification?) of the ego rather than seek
redemption in humility, let dying echoes in
the shadow of a child's soul feed imagination,
relying on a custom built God for salvation
should the politics of disintegration become
a serious moral issue

Growing old, I haunt that place of shadows,
greet them as old acquaintances, even try
pretending we were friends, though forced
to confess I'd sought them out for own ends
but keen to make amends (no idea how)
mindful of nature's gentler surrounds, inner
eye blinking at children chasing after a fragile
mortality, asking questions not asked before
when answers seemed far less important than
actions according to whatever rule of thumb
most convenient at the time, best explained or
excused as 'meant well' or (better still) for
the greater good of next generations warned
against hurting butterflies

Valley of shadows, where words left unsaid
gorge on things left undone - and spit us out

BEYOND GLASTONBURY

Long, winding road, pockets of death
like loud, angry signposts

Flowers and cards left for passers-by
to test their quality of life

Foot down, anxious for home comforts
in safe, unpaid-for armchairs

Braking sharply to let hedgehogs cross
our (guilty?) consciences

Pop song on the radio, glaring memories
of a muddy Glastonbury

Homing in at last on fuel bills, junk mail
and other endearments

Weary of negotiating loud, angry sunsets
sign-posting heaven

Feet up. Glastonbury and home comforts,
a sinking in armchairs

DANCER AT THE EDGE OF TIME

On a custom-built stage reaching out
to mind and soul anxious to express
our reasons for being here despite
smouldering coals of body language,
petty potholes of pretty speech
(or signing) - for any language can
but brush the surface of those nether
regions of self…wherein we rage
at being misunderstood

Now meek, mild; now grown wild,
this dance of a lifetime they paid
a high price to see who have
summoned me here (for a private
viewing only) hoping to be shown
the various steps between right
and wrong – and in so doing,
learn something, at least, about
live art

Gliding with grace, gesturing a plea
to be acknowledged (better still,
recognized) by an inner eye that's
too often inclined to remain shut
than be made to choose a path we'd
much rather ignore. Dancer takes
a bow. Performance over, task all
but ended; art's love affair with life
lent new meaning, purpose

So let's learn, no time to rehearse;
the next move ours

ODE TO A HOMOPHOBE

You parade your macho like a trophy
and frequently abuse gay men
but if so confident in your sexuality
why this crass overreaction?

You say gay people are sad, sick cases,
at the very least immoral,
yet you go to church, sing His praises
(and expect Him to be grateful?)

You say being gay is a mortal sin,
love to take the moral high…
yet what less right gay men and women
to love and be loved till they die?

Gay people need to give truth a name
and learn to give it substance;
Homophobes would never dare the same
for fear of exposing their ignorance

We are all God's children, the churches cry,
each worthy of His love and our own;
Yet time after time their holy leaders lie,
leave gay people to pray alone

The century is changing it has to be said,
a War on Terror all around
and while one homophobe wishes us dead,
it is a war without end

PART 4

GAY IS OK, SAYS WHO?

GAY IS OK, SAYS WHO?

If the world is, oh, so politically correct,
why should it matter if people suspect we're gay?
(How many fathers, how many mothers
ask if their sons, daughters, have same sex lovers?)
Whatever happened to just being straight
about who it is we are and what it is we stand for?
(Aren't we protected now by legislation?)
Gay, we're told, is ok - so why any hesitation?
Yes, I know it was in the news today,
about someone brutally killed for being openly gay
but that was a cultural, ethnic blip or flaw,
all tied up with old religion-speak and tribal law,
nothing to do with the likes of us trying to
rationalise a twenty-first century equality of sorts.
We can legislate for a common humanity
but that doesn't mean to say its bigots will keep
an open mind so, no, we shouldn't wait
to tell the world say we're gay…or how else
this world, its way, expect to find?

How long before one voice worldwide
ceasing to pause at a three-letter word?

LET THE MUSIC PLAY
(For Mike & Trevor)

I creep up on you as time passes by;
you sense my presence but unsure
how or why it should make you feel
different from the way you thought
you were (as told) not so many years
before, when childhood games took
their cue from history, the mysteries
of adulthood waiting in the wings
for its mortal gamut to be run

I seize upon your senses as they wake
to the challenges of peer pressure,
parental expectations, private desires
lighting fires in the heart, ambition
conspiring with aspiration to indulge
the mind its appetite for a fate far better
than mapped out at school or around
the kitchen table. Yet, I too, am here
and you less able to suss me out?

I will pluck at your nerve strings until
you recognize the tune I play and let
it loose on heart, mind, body and soul
though (for a while at least) you share it
with no one, unsure how. Now, choose.
Play out the most beautiful song you will
ever hear or let me go, follow a safer
course, give ambition (or convention?)
a stronger, louder (better?) voice

Only, listen to the music and let it play,
this gene that says, "I'm gay."

NO STORYBOOK HERO

When I listen to the waves,
they always tell the same stories
I used to hear from leafy choirs
long, long ago…how one day
I'd be riding a white horse
to fame and glory. Only, life never
took me that way, but in other
directions…despite objections from
alter ego, friends and family;
I wasn't meant be a hero of the kind
that's rides out storms, surfs
giant waves, climbs snowy peaks,
charges to the rescue (bugles blaring)
in time to save the goodies from
the baddies the way they manage it
in the best movies and books;
Instead, life found another role for me,
an Ordinary Joe in the street,
always trying to make the best of things,
struggling to make ends meet;
nothing to lose, everything to prove
because I'm gay and not cut out
for heroics. So let the world do its worst
and knock me down, I can but
bounce right back like a circus clown
or a child's wobbly toy (so do I hear
applause, it has to be better than tears?)
get on with my life as best I can
(take it on the chin, like a 'real' man)
play my part…from the heart
for who I am, no hero out of stories
heard long, long ago, just a very
Ordinary Joe fighting old prejudices,

siding with the trees against a world
telling stories to its children who
(hopefully) know better than to listen

SPRING, ON CUE

On a fence watching
lambs playing without a care
in the world;
Burden of love starting
to lift, rays of sunshine breaking
through clouds;
Cart horses in the next field
canter by, chasing after the same
pretty butterfly;
In spring leaves, glimpse
fledgling bravehearts egged on
by tree spirits;
A bee humming our tune
darts away, just as your hand
reaches for mine;
Time to jump down, take
our cue from country blessings,
count our own;
Moving on, spring in
each step, pausing only to kiss
beside busy hedgerows;
Reach the highway, jump
In the car, gay people happier
than once we were

POSTCARDS FROM THE EDGE
(For Brian H.)

Driven to the naked edge of a snake pit, peering in,
all but poised to leap, defy demons on the brain
constantly jeering because I'm gay, weary of family
and friends urging no surrender to a growing desire
for my own gender, thus acknowledging this, a sexual
identity integral to every other part of me, although
those parts the same, no less true for being honest,
drawn to home truths haunting me since that dawn
I confronted myself for who I am, even as I continued
to perpetuate a sham of being straight (taught a sin,
at the very least a crime - to be gay)

With each new day, subtle shifts of opinion, even in
a fickle media, then legislation intended to give gay
men and women a kinder freedom

I stood alone, scared, desperate to end these lies,
half lies, a creeping among shadows like a thief
seeking a love I dare not own, so strong history's
ties intent on binding me martyr-like to convention's
Cross of Convenience

Now, breaking free?

Oh, to let history see I am my own person, refuse to
be made subservient to stereotype! Even so, never
my intention to offend those who have meant me well
(if brought me here, in tears, wondering whether to
let the neighbourhood bigots carry on breaking backs
with rods for straws or set about making repairs)

Down to us. So, no more snake pits and self-pity
but a life in the light of gay love, proudly

FIRST CHRISTMAS

I could hear cock robin's song in the air;
at a window I watched first snowflakes fall,
missing you so and wishing we could share
that gift of love at Christmas to us all

In the distance I could hear bells ringing,
a sound to fill this lonely heart with cheer;
at my own front door, an angel's singing
calling on Christmas to bring its love here

In the window's reflection, next to mine,
I watched a sad face break into a smile,
aching heart soaring, a white dove divine,
lifting the snowflakes like a wedding veil

I raced to the front door and flung it wide…
a gay love redeemed, our first Christmastide

THREE LITTLE WORDS

Three little words, all I had to say
but dare not, day after day…

My heart ached each time I tried
so crossed my fingers and lied…

It hurt, each time you looked at me
as if urging I speak, break free…

Yet three little words I could not say
though loving you more each day…

My soul cried out in bleakest despair
so I shut my ears, tried not to hear…

I died when you heaped praise on me,
the coward in me you could not see…

Three little words, all I had to say
but dare not, day after day…

There had to be more to life than this
growing empathy with Judas…

To family, friends, at last I came true;
no problem, love won through…

Three little words, I'm so proud to say
day after day, 'I am gay'

CONFESSIONS OF A SANDMAN

Met a man one day...
a stranger (yet not so) was he
and handsome, blue eyes
like a watercolour sea;
He paused and spoke words
I longed to hear, this handsome
man with eyes like stars
on a midnight clear;
He laughed, told me to relax
and not be afraid, this handsome
man, eyes as sharp as any
kitchen blade;
He took my hand, suggested
we walk a while, this handsome
man with laughing eyes
and a wine stain smile;
Under a sycamore, he paused
to stroke my hair, this handsome
man with sparkling eyes
I had no cause to fear;
Oh, the bliss of his kiss when
it came, this hot-blooded devil
with teasing eyes who would
not give his name;
Mouth to mouth, he brought me
to my knees in the grass, eyes like
raindrops on a fading flower
restored to life...

We made love till clerics charged us,
spiriting away passion's gaze opening
my eyes

THAT FIRST TIME

That first time you touched me, I knew myself;
that first time you kissed me, I found myself

That first time we made love my heart took flight
to a sunny blue heaven once as dark as night

That first time we lay, spent, in each other's arms
I heard Pan's flute, succumbed to its charms

That first time we quarrelled and resolved to part,
I discovered the grief of a broken heart...

That first time we shared humility's loving cup,
I discovered the ecstasy of making up...

That first time we tested the world's prejudices,
I was proud to be gay, the more so to be yours

STREET KISSES

Street kisses shared
far, far sweeter than wine;
twin souls bared

Heart pounding, scared,
you lent your body to mine;
street kisses shared

For years we'd cared,
though the world draw a line;
twin souls bared

Once we despaired,
most people quick to malign
street kisses shared

We hadn't dared
give even the slightest sign;
twin souls shared

Let them see we're gay,
the love in our faces shine;
street kisses shared,
twin souls bared

A SONG FOR GAY LOVERS
(For Gary & Michael)

It doesn't matter that we're gay,
our love is pure;
whatever people say, it will endure

It doesn't matter that we're gay,
happiness is ours;
day by day, winging heaven's towers

It doesn't matter that we're gay,
time is on our side;
ebb or flow, let golden hours decide

It doesn't matter that we're gay,
we can dream too;
come what may, we'll see it through

It doesn't matter that we're gay,
our love is pure;
whatever people say, we will endure

GENESIS

There's a poem I've often tried to write
about the way his hair blows in a breeze
and his face almost vanishes from sight
but for a wicked laughter in the eyes

There's a poem I've often tried to write
about the way his voice eases my pain
like a balm to sores, moon to wintry night,
sunshine filtering through a summer rain

There's a poem I've often tried to write
about the way his hugs near break my heart
and how, as his arms are holding me tight,
it aches for knowing we must quickly part

There's a friend for whom I've often begun
poems I know he'll wish I'd not written…

SOMETIMES

Sometimes I regret being gay,
take long walks in the rain…
pausing now and then to ponder
puddles, wonder why I envy
the conventional person living
a conventional life in a two up,
two down, plagued by in-laws,
wife and 2.5 children

Sometimes I regret being gay,
take long walks by the canal…
pausing now and then to watch
geese flying high and free, just
as I yearn to be but feel trapped
in a cage where society would
have me stay though it dare not
give public voice to the thought
or risk being taken to court

Sometimes I regret being gay
take long walks on the heath…
pausing now and then to chat
with this and that person (some
gay, some not) about the weather,
global warming, War on Terror,
so much poverty in the world,
and how we should be glad - for
a fine day and the way we are

Sometimes, being gay is a burden
till, with you, I lay my body down

BEING GAY, BEING STRAIGHT

When I told a straight mate I'm gay,
he shrugged and walked away;
I watched him go, heart sinking, thinking
maybe better I'd said nothing;
Yet it felt so good for having found a way
(the words weren't easy to say);
A sense of breaking free left me on a high
but we were mates and I'd lived a lie;
I could scarcely imagine his hurt, his anger
at discovering I was a stranger
and wished I'd told him years ago. I tried
but I hadn't the nerve, so I lied;
Being straight with folks was easy after that
but I missed seeing my old mate;
Weeks later, we met by chance at a local bar
ignored each other for over an hour
before he came over, slammed down a mug
and lifted me up in a bear hug;
Sometimes he'll even crack gay jokes when
in company or on our own...
because he feels so comfortable with me
(isn't that how it should be?);
I tell jokes about straight folks, fair's fair;
we live different lives but still care

Isn't that what mates are for?

BELOVED INVADER

When you invaded my body,
passion, heat and desire
throbbing at the very fingertips,
I thought I was surely dying
to come so close to heaven
on an earth ravaged by pain,
even the flowers hurting from
a steady fall of acid rain

When you invaded my body.
passion, heat and desire
foaming at a full, sweet mouth,
I thought I was surely blessed
to feel the arms of an angel
embracing me with such love
and more, in a world so haunted
by poverty, hunger, terror

When you invaded my body,
passion heat and desire
coaxing me to glorious orgasm,
I learned to know myself,
freed at last from fear and doubt,
like a flower whose petals
stayed shut, until nature's need
to come out…

Oh, beloved invader, but for you,
no poem of mine would ring true

A CHRISTMAS BLESSING

They said it didn't matter I'm gay,
seemed glad for me when I found you,
accepted us as a couple, for who
and what we are - and we were happy;
Days, months, passed and nothing
happened to spoil our idyll - but as
autumn passed into winter…
we noticed a change in people;
As hearts and minds began to focus
on Christmas… was it only in
my imagination that they looked away?
Everyone began asking everyone else
what they were doing for Christmas,
except us. Whenever we ventured
to suggest this 'n' that… 'Oh, we'd love
to have you, of course but, sorry…
a full house this year. Besides, you know
how some old people feel about gays
and we don't want to spoil grandma's
Christmas do we?' (Said most sincerely).
So we happily anticipated a quiet, loving
time, just the two of us

Just days before Christmas, a phone call
from your grandmother to say how she was
looking forward to seeing you. 'Oh, and
your partner too of course. It was different
in my day. Few people had the courage
to be openly gay…'

GAY SONNETEER

We had little choice; it was not a time
for such as you and I, our love to own;
the law said we had committed a crime;
our families would shun us and disown

Swinging sixties, a sex revolution,
but not for such as we, still in our teens,
learning in school about evolution…
yearning in bed to escape what it means

I felt like a ghost in my own lifetime,
clinging to conventions, scared to let go,
seeking of sonnets a comfort in rhyme,
Dead-Man-Walking in another's shadow

I looked into my soul, learned to trust it,
a gay life on track, theme for a sonnet

FAST TRACKING

You dived under my top,
tongue on nipples aching with desire;
hands at my jeans would not stop,
my whole being on fire

I longed to respond, could not
(for too long told it's wrong, obscene)
as you invaded me with your heat,
pulled my jeans down

My heart tore like an express
along twisting tracks of denial, regret,
embracing years of loneliness, pain,
on a rack of ages-old guilt

Slowly, I let go all hype
imprinted on my heart, soul, brain;
rose above the stereotype,
learned to live again

Once mere pieces of clay,
we discovered sex, no truths held back;
though some protest, as they may,
let them to their own lives look

BRING ME THE HEAD OF AN HONEST MAN

The first time you touched me
was by chance (was it not?) yet in my head
began a dance more seductive than Salome's
for John's head; my legs caved in to its spell
and I had to sit down, the dance driving me mad
with a desire I hadn't acknowledged before,
closeted in corners of a mind unable to come
to terms with all that's poised there, desperate
to leap on the back of thoughts told inappropriate
for a child, now lighting a fire driving me mad
with passion, longing to take this dancer in arms
desperate for the intimacy of body to body,
cheek to cheek, declaring ourselves lovers.
Yet, how may I desire a lover of my own sex?
It cannot be so, cannot be right if it is true,
all I have ever heard said at home, school, work;
Ah, but how can I deny feelings like this, as
much a part of me as a father's hug, mother's kiss,
brother's playful knock-about or being teased
by a best mate? How to take the dancer as I find
without denying family and friends peace of mind,
explaining how the person they perceive is but a shell
this inner self must leave - to live a life that's true,
shedding veils a body would hide, seizing alter ego
by the head, kissing its lips, setting the soul's tongue
free to seek, explore, where it never dared before?
Dance done. Your fair head in my hands
no trophy, but a prize, dearly won

LIVING OVER THE PAWNBROKER'S SHOP

He was leaning against a lamp-post, flickering,
almost dead. He demanded a cigarette. I said
I didn't smoke. I'd have walked on but then he
asked the time. On impulse, I confessed I'd
left my watch with a pawnbroker, times were hard;
I saw he understood, although by now the light
had all but died. He told me he had no money or
place to go since his wife had discovered his appetite
for other men. She had kept their house (and kids),
taking care to have the locks changed, find a good
lawyer to take her side against someone working
extra hours to pay the mortgage, keep her happy, see
the kids through university, mother-in-law in clover
because she had never liked him anyway, thought
daughter could do better, though not a bad father
she'd grudgingly admit but...so what? Daughter taken
for better, for worse (worse as far as she could see);
Better by far to make a clean break, no matter how
things might turn out for a husband and dad, just so
long as life seen to be fair to the mother (views often
aired whenever souls bared on chat-time TV).

Street lamp died. He became but a shadow though
a light in the eyes told me all I needed to know;
A family man he may have been but now, like me,
he clearly hungered for that intimacy long since
short-changed him by a society anxious to preserve
its integrity. I took him back to my place for sex.
By dawn, he'd gone. On lilac sheets, a stain to remind
me (when will I ever learn?) that men cruising
are much like watches on show in a pawnbroker's
window, waiting to be redeemed

JACK-IN-THE-BOX

Once, I'd make up life as I went along
with Jack, my invisible friend;
He was always there for me, teasing
but never passing judgement;
Only Jack knew I was gay, a teenager
in love with the boy next door
whose mother thought fate meant me
for her daughter; cue for laughter
from Jack , no matter my shame for
going along with the farce, even
asking the daughter on a date because
her brother is her mate's boyfriend
and we'd all hang out; I'd grab every
chance to be close to him, feel his
breath on me, a finger brushing mine,
getting higher on the sheer poetry
of his voice than any music, dancing
or wine

At his door, I'd kiss her briefly, ignoring
the pain in her eyes, her best friend
embracing my love nearby, lips meant
(surely?) for mine, a place in his life,
stealing my passion, usurping my dreams
and (worse) making them real while I
dare not reveal how I feel, Jack at my ear
saying less harm in lies than let truth
run its course, better play charades than
drop the mask, show a private face;
(Oh, to feel his heat and taste his kiss!)
She knew, of course, yet kept saying
she loved me and I fear she did, though
Jack knows I never said the words

she longed to hear nor let her passion
get the better of us, he at my ear
saying, no matter…wasn't as if I didn't
care for her at all

Youth long past, stumbling into maturity,
I finally told everyone I am gay;
Most people stood by me, gave me a hug,
said it didn't matter, sexuality less
important than a sound mind, good heart
by far; most people, that is, except the guy
who used to be the boy next door;
But I don't need him any more and Jack's
gone too, nor is gay love a make-believe
dent on the pillow next to me, invisible lips
mouthing words of desire…for I am out
in the world, high on a love and friendship
restoring my integrity, replacing regret
for an unrequited youth with a self-respect
and honesty; the man I used to be, scared
of reality and behaving badly, finally ready
for a sexual identity demanding I accept
responsibility for it

MIRROR, MIRROR

Once, studying my reflection,
I didn't like what I saw,
engaged me in conversation
about being gay - and more

I confessed to feeling guilty,
couldn't help how I feel,
people making me feel dirty
for being me, getting real

No need, said my reflection,
you're as good as them;
people raising any objection
to being gay - their problem

But I was taught it is a sin
during formative years,
kept on the outside peeping in,
obliged to hide my tears

Don't cry, said my reflection,
you're as good as them;
people raising any objection
to being gay - their problem

Once, studying my reflection,
you liked what you saw,
engaged me in conversation
about being gay - and more

Now, no longer feeling guilty
or made to feel out of place
but the dear love to inspire me
written on your face

LIFE-FORCE

Once, I met a young man by a river
beneath a leafy awning of willow;
in a summer's heat I could but shiver
nor would my lips even frame a 'hello'

We glimpsed a kingfisher on graceful wing
a flash of breast the colour of his eyes
and, just as one, we watched its descending,
so too did we welcome nature's surprise

We found a voice and let it lay us down,
river anxious we should hear a story
about desire, sex, and how seeds once sown
and nurtured aspire to nature's glory

Come twilight, we went our separate ways,
glimpses of gay love, a life-force always

NOTHING EVER QUITE THE SAME AGAIN

We sat opposite each other
on a fast train to heaven;
Me, trying not to look too hard
in his direction;
He, struggling to resist a glance
too often in mine

I couldn't focus on my book
for the flames in his hair
torching every page, setting this
heart of mine on fire
with desire, a growing hunger
to kiss a stranger

In mischievous sea-blue eyes
I stripped naked and swam
to a far, sandy shore, the colour
of his shirt, sprawled there
in the sun till he laid his body
down, next to mine

One hand caressed my cheek,
the other stroked my thigh
then he leaned and kissed me,
our arms entwining…
his skin like satin, sex hard,
bold, exciting

I missed my station, didn't care;
As fate would have it
he did the same, till we came
to the end of the line
and he told me his name,
I told him mine

Homeward bound on another train,
nothing ever quite the same again…

ODE TO A SCHOOL CAP

On a pebbly shore observing the sea
about to snatch an abandoned deckchair,
I wonder…do you ever think of me,
snatching at my cap, fingers in my hair?

A breeze, come evening, laughing at us,
shadow fingers masturbating, a bliss
sure to catch us out under summer skies,
a passing cloud witnessing our first kiss

No one ever guessed why you went away
across a sea that calls me with your voice;
much as I loved you, implored you to stay,
each kiss but postponing a time of choice

Not ready then to tell the world I'm gay,
left letting its tides snatch my cap away

A CHRISTMAS STORY

Standing close to me in the queue,
buttocks pressing on my groin;
My sex aroused, I could but surf
waves of desire, tumbling like blond
highlights in the long brown hair;
If I'd stuck out my tongue, it would
have brushed the pale neck gracing
a denim shirt collar like down
of an angel's wing making night moves
on my heart's reawakening;
Moving forward in the queue till just
us pair, a lump in my throat hard
and throbbing like an erection
(that, too) as in craters of a full moon
I made frantic love…to you;
A taxi pulled up alongside us, your turn
to vanish into a darker side of town;
You casually asked if I'd care to share
and I could but nod, follow those
highlights in your hair…wherever;
In the back seat, leg pressing against
mine, we gladly revealed our names - and
more. It was time, we both knew,
to stop playing games, answer a question
in the wing mirror's eyes as the taxi
pulled up at your door. It was now
or never. I yielded to temptation, said 'yes'
without hesitation; though it be but
a one-night stand, I was hooked, my place
in your bed long since booked…
our Christmas goose all but cooked

WHO HASN'T HEARD THE FAT LADY SING?

Fat lady in black, singing
life is pointless;
Man in the pink, promising
love and peace

Fat lady in black singing
about time wasted;
Man in the pink, promising
peace and love

Fat lady in black, singing
some home truths;
Man in the pink, promising
love and peace

Fat lady in black, singing
about making amends;
Man in the pink, promising
peace and love

Fat lady in black, singing
of life's perversities;
Man in the pink, promising
love and peace

Fat lady in black, dying
to keep us apart;
Man in the pink, a triangle
over his heart

LINES ON IMMORTALITY

You wear jeans, your shirt is white;
hair, a crown of gold in the soft twilight
like a god in fields spring green,
the most beautiful man I've ever seen

I watch in awe, rooted to the spot
as you chat with flowers, this tree, that bird
in a voice as sweet as Pan's own flute,
the most beautiful sound I've ever heard

I catch your eye, rush into your arms,
savour full, moist lips crushed against mine,
a murmuring of centuries-old charms
turning midwinter on my tongue into wine

Too soon you leave, yet sweeter my agony
for a love that lends us immortality…

PART 5

HALLOWEEN LANDSCAPE

HALLOWEEN LANDSCAPE

Bruised faces hanging
low over grass that's glowing
like Halloween candles

Lightning severing
familiar heads come twilight's
makeshift guillotine

Sounds like violins
mourning the dead of Auschwitz
where songbirds sleep

A long, hard weeping
at leafy doors deaf to the frantic
beating of twin fists

The blustering fury
of dark angels in freefall, like
gay bashers celebrating

This world, a ghastly place
for Salem's best, whom history
let do their worst

Storm passes, returning
our ghosts to that open prison
we call 'conscience'

OUT OF EDEN

Once, Adam and Eve walked in a garden,
left Big Brother masturbating in bed,
in time to observe a dawn's playful sun
a fine angel dust quickly spill and spread

As sure as it covered a tearful sky,
so it smothered Eve's torment and despair
as kinder memories in the mind's eye
replaced sad, bleak, cruel images there

At one with birdsong, roses, nature's joys
trumpeting second chances, a fresh start;
once counted among the world's reject toys,
now come to life, given hope, taking heart

Better world in a better person's head,
Big Brother left masturbating in bed…

TIME AND AGAIN

Time and again, lights go out
all over the world;
Time and again, brave men
and women risk all…to
turn them back on

Time and again, the dogs of war
tear into the world;
Time and again, skilled men
and women dare…to
attempt repair

Time and again, bringers of peace
promise us eternity;
Time and again, fine men
and women give all…to
see us through

Time and again, broken promises
litter the earth;
Time and again, sons and daughters,
friends and neighbours…will
pick up the pieces

Time and again, we'll give thanks
all over the world;
Time and again, our brave men
and women must wish…we
would try harder

THE RHETORIC OF BLAME

So young they stood on the edge of war,
strutting courage and dreaming of glory,
no idea of the carnage gone before,
rewriting, in blood, their nation's story

Heads high, happy to answer duty's call,
emblems of faith in the wind, flags unfurled,
no one suspecting how many might fall
or prayers unanswered around the world

Victory, when it came fell on time's sword
at the eleventh hour, day, month, 1918;
No action-replay, we gave God our word,
only to break it again and again…

We speak of peace, while finding excuses
for a blame game, gambling all our futures

NOW IRAQ, WHAT NEXT?

A pile of rubble, all that's left of a home
once lived, once loved

Bloody bodies and belongings, scattered
like discarded toys

By the road, angry hands make light work
of planting bombs

In hearts the world over, politics on trial for
crimes against humanity

At whose grave next, left kneeling, asking
bitter questions?

On the head of whose leader next, heaping
a rage to live?

To whose God next run scared, praying any
future mark us well?

No matter history next rewritten, in vain its
books kept clean

POINTING TO ARMAGEDDON

Three desperate men take their lives;
(no room for tears)

An act of war, the commander says;
(empathy with propaganda)

Typical political comment, on martyrs
(predisposed to tragedy)

Futures coloured by shades of orange
(flames in a War on Terror)

Resentment, spreads across the world
(like avian flu…)

Better to be safe than sorry, as they say
(in the Corridors of Power)

Lords of a dying planet, in summit talks
(to best each other)

Terror, continuing to feed on injustice
(blindfolds shared out)

Children of the good earth, seeking better
(of self-styled betters)

Peace and hope, pointing to Armageddon
(Guantanamo Bay)

[June 11th 2006]

YEARS ON

Let us all remember, years on,
loved ones who passed away
one July 7th in London

Injured, bereaved, battles won
so terror shall not hold sway;
let us all remember, years on

A mother, father, daughter, son…
deaths, in our lives, parts to play
one July 7th in London

On fanatics, a martyr's light shone
though humanity too has a say;
let us all remember, years on

Where hate and despair raging on,
find hope in the cold light of day,
one July 7th in London

Love, if sorely tried and put upon,
will always find its way;
Let us all remember, years on,
one July 7th in London

Note: This villanelle was written shortly after the London bombings, July 7th 2005.

HOME GROWN

A cry in the night, could be
human or beast,
sneaking past the Old Man
like a snake

A stalking star, fallen upon
its victim?

Feet dead, thought paralysed
by indecision;
Does someone need help, but
in what direction?

Probably a cat, trapped in that
dark alley's jaws

Quiet. Blood rediscovering its
everyday route;
Mind functioning sufficiently
to agree inaction

Body heading for home, as if
never disturbed

A cry in the night, marking us
for human or beast;
Heart beating madly, madness
everywhere

Of global terrors, none greater
than home grown

LISTENING FOR THE DODO

Come dawn,
a knocking at the heart;
High noon,
time to make a start

Suicide robots
input to blow the mind;
G8 reports,
the media-friendly kind

Four o'clock,
might as well have tea;
TV News,
homing in on misery

Twilight's gold
argues we're too old;
Sunset's flood
warns rivers of blood

Faiths must clash
and gods must weep?
Sandman says
we're in far too deep

Broken sleep,
world won't play fair;
Knock, knock…
who (or what) is there?

KATRINA'S WAKE

Jazz city's played out
(floods of tears))

People yelling for help
(who's listening?)

Others dying of thirst
('Cumbyar, Lord')

Bodies in the sewage
(songs of silence)

Looting on the streets
(no one to stop it?)

Grabbing clean water
(no matter how)

Tales told of survival
(water into wine)

Press conferences…
(help arriving?)

Ghosts at the Gulf…
scared of waking

ONCE, NEW ORLEANS

Once, left frozen and hungry
on a rooftop;
Once, watching flood waters
rising, rising…

Once, for friends and family
a fading hope;
Once, for an imminent rescue,
fat chance

Once, TV audiences wringing
their hands;
Once, we were all equal under
the same flag

Once, we could look forward to
better tomorrows;
Once, it was one for all and all
for one

Once, it would take more than a
hurricane to…
Ah, but we can't blame Katrina
for everything

At least the Superdome makeover
is looking good

MAELSTROM

No crueller wisdom
nor faith more blindly placed
than martyrdom

Life's tragic outcome,
love's sacred trust misplaced;
no crueller wisdom

No prouder kingdom
better served by want and waste
than martyrdom

By a beating drum,
each sound heartbeat replaced;
no crueller wisdom

No glory closer come
to grief, by holy words defaced,
than martyrdom

Magnificent maelstrom,
supposedly to God's door traced;
no crueller wisdom
than martyrdom

LONG WINTER, LONELY SPRING

Once, I met a greybeard in early spring
who asked me to walk with him by the sea,
related how he'd staked everything
on greed and good old fashioned jealousy

Envied, arm in arm with fame, fortune, love,
this was never enough, he needed more,
made false friends, subtle enemies, above
and below his place on life's wooden stair

Pushing, shoving, kicking, he'd made progress,
only vaguely sensing loved ones drop away,
reaching for what he'd heard called happiness
despite anything wiser folks might say

We parted, his cheeks wet with a tide's tears,
spring but a bedtime story in his ears

SOLDIERING ON

Seconds before dawn,
caressed by a velvety dark,
seduced by its charms;
safe in Someone's arms,
stuff of dreams

Seconds before dawn,
taste and smell of silence
invading the senses;
poetry in Someone's arms,
myth of dreams

Seconds before dawn,
laughing among old gods
before answering
a wake-up call to arms,
save our dreams

Suddenly, dawn strikes
the first blow in a battle royal
and we must get real,
senses alerted to terror's
war on dreams

From mortality, poor protection;
in dreams, redemption?

A STITCH IN TIME

Oh, but to nurture such beautiful dreams
of an end to all wars, a lasting peace…
in fair lands falling apart at the seams,
their pain, like acid rain, falling on us

Save a longing for its dreams to be real,
humankind despairs…as scenes on TV
feed its fears, encourage wounds to congeal,
for all they command our soap box pity

Nor will History look too unkindly
on a tit-for-tat culture prevailing…
to save face with that same hypocrisy
arms dealers kept busy consecrating

Oh, for a turn at the heart's loom weaving
one stitch in a peace of the world's making

RED

Shades of red, as colouring world religions,
writing political agendas

When I open my heart, I see red - the colour
of your courage

When I open my eyes, I see red - the colour
of my pain

Red, too, shades of our last sunset before you
left do your duty far away

Red also, on the flag that covered your coffin
as a band played you home

Red, these eyes, that have no tears left for us
but must see their way clear

Red, these lips that will never kiss yours again
but must reassure generations

When I open my heart, I see red - the colour
of your blood

When I open my eyes, I see red - the colour
of my rage

Shades of red, as colouring humankind's boast
of a common humanity

WAITING FOR RAIN

Beautiful day,
sun shining brightly;
curtains open, lie-in
well-deserved

Clear blue sky,
birds winging lightly;
breakfast headlines,
assault on apathy

Clouds forming,
could be up for rain?
Cows lying down,
native instinct

Missiles making
splashes on soft targets,
drumming up more
makeshift coffins

CRY, WOLF

Humanity's heat run cold
among the graves of its dead,
a history all but told

Love, to lust auctioned, sold
to dark angels seduced, misled;
humanity's heat run cold

War, a wolf to the sheepfold,
poised to rear its shadowy head;
a history all but told

Kinder souls into slavery sold,
made to make Big Brother's bed;
humanity's heat run cold

Prejudice, a lasting mould
cast in the shape of a wolf's head;
a history all but told

See climate change unfold,
hope on crumbs of integrity fed;
humanity's heat run cold,
a history all but told

WAKING UP TO GODOT

Twilight, sword
of the gods;
Silence, a cocoon
of sleep

Dreams, making good
past mistakes;
(Ghosts, making sport
with us?)

Hint of dawn, cracks
in our defences;
Truth, buried under
excuses

Daylight, armour
of the gods;
Come noon, world
fighting back

TOUCHLINES

On a touchline we'd follow our seasons
across a playing field of changing skies,
blowing tin whistles on Nature's reasons
for appealing against humankind's lies

Never content to be sidelined for long,
we entered the game, devising new rules,
tin whistles drowning out even birdsong
for humankind's ego, its own fate seals

Not only cheating and spoiling the game
but convinced even God is on our side
(private sponsor by any other name?);
where nature rules, His leave to override

Crossing touchlines, ready to turn deaf ears
to Nature's cry that it's for us it fears

REFLECTIONS ON A WET NIGHT

All our yesterdays gone
so let's make the most of today;
Don't leave me alone
but take my hand, for together
we shall find our way
through this maze of wet streets,
though faces haunt us,
words taunting us like reflections
of half dead dreams in
puddles filled with hazy lamplight
that would thwart us at
every step we dare, each look we
care to chance, hoping
for answers or (at the very least)
potential for escaping
a nightmare hounding our every
breath, move, clinging
to each other like drowning souls
in a cruel sea anxiously
anticipating that such as we might
survive its rushing to
judgement, even emerge the better
for having fought off
its ghosts, run the ghastly gamut,
a Hall of Mirrors
created for the delight of old gods
hiding in moon craters
rather than risk being exposed for
such puerile jokers
as those from whom we're licking
our wounds on a wet night,
almost ready to take the dawn
into our confidence

> though its chorus lead where it may,
> heaven's descent at the ear,
> answer to a gay couple's prayer

GOD'S METAPHOR

Passive spectators to war,
the last tree left standing evergreen;
God's metaphor

Like Adam tested before,
by the world's dark intentions unseen,
passive spectators to war

Eve called out for a whore
by the likes of whom we've never seen;
God's metaphor

Lights at the kitchen door
hinting at a feast for the television screen,
passive spectators to war

Snakes in the grass and more
leaving trails to ambition's lust obscene;
God's metaphor

Dare we who know the score
let one coin outshine a leaf's dawn sheen?
Passive spectators to war…
God's metaphor

NATURE'S WAY

Sunset, but last blushes
for our shortcomings

Mosquitoes, like missiles
homing in like scalpels

Heaven heals the wound,
(God pundits divided)

By dawn, subtle birdsong;
State of the Union

Clouds, wary foot soldiers
at the ballot box

High noon, no retreat even
for polar bears

Sycamore droppings, angels
attending Armageddon

Twilight, wrapping it all up
to look pretty

Stars, left to take the moral
high ground

LAST STAND

On the last day of the year in a world
content to wear its heart on one fair sleeve,
to whom will it fall, a prevailing word,
sure to let Mother Nature safely grieve?

At altar or alter ego convene…
to give love, peace and truth a final say,
listen, agree and act on what they mean
or let dissent, as always, win the day?

Must wars fund the food of a peace we crave
that manna from churches will not provide
since barely enough, their own kind to save,
(the rest might as well already have died)

On our last day in the world, spare a thought
for those fighting to survive, gay or straight

COME TWILIGHT'S SWORD

I was lying in my bed
when an angel came and said,
'Won't you come with me?'

No time to frame a word
under threat of twilight's sword,
nor barely able to see

Scared, I shook my head
but the angel laughed and said,
'You must come with me.'

I explained I couldn't leave,
loved ones tugging at my sleeve;
from the angel, no reprieve

Near heaven, I looked back,
world on Man's customised rack
crying out to me

Did the angel release my hand
at Nature's hysterical command
its trees and poets go free?

I'll never know, for I awoke;
Behind dawn's veil, a lark spoke,
'Do your best for me.'

PART 6

BUSINESS AS USUAL

BUSINESS AS USUAL

Pavements littered with eggshells
(politically correct)

Someone waving a Big Issue
(Equal Ops suspect)

M-25 a nightmare
(car is king)

Beggar and dog at the supermarket
(outside, looking in)

Bag lady resting on a park bench
(move along, security alert)

Blind man waiting at the kerbside
(ably assisted by a pickpocket)

Could be a suicide bomber, see?
(looks sort of foreign to me)

Lovers sharing well used needles
(so what *about* HIV?)

School kid mugged for a mobile
(someone call the local rag…)

Say slim, think sexy, be beautiful
(gorging on a glossy mag)

Sales at every High Street store
(credit card freefall)

Dog chasing cat down the street
(Business as usual)

CUSTOMER CARE

What I'd forgotten I couldn't quite place
a second time I walked into the shop;
suddenly, I could feel Suspicion's gaze
tearing into my flesh, nor would it stop

I half-turned, saw a pair of glaring eyes
watching my every innocent move,
their owner summoning help to comprise
an ugly trio, my guilt poised to prove

Scared, I left, no word or challenge spoken
until He who still kept me in his sights
ran after me, escorted me back, said to open
my bag, prove I had paid, waive my rights

Honesty upheld, now suspicion free…
Small change, the rape of my integrity

<u>Note</u>: I was wrongly accused of shoplifting at a Somerfield store in Kentish Town, October 2006. It was a very traumatic experience.

WITNESS FOR THE PROSECUTION

I've seen kids on London's streets
beg coins for bus fares or worse,
steal a blind woman's purse,
mock a one-legged man's affliction
then yell "Persecution!" at passing
coppers trying to do their duty
by some council estate community
suffering daily from the traumas
of kids without conscience, let alone
good manners (fat chance!)
leading the locals a rare old dance,
skipping school whenever,
drinking, smoking this 'n' that,
pleading victims of society
should they happen to get caught,
held up as poor specimens
found slipped through Propriety's net
no matter colour or creed,
this new breed of wide, street urchin
whose familiarity with rights
racism and other discrimination
would be admirable - were
it not, invariably, used as a weapon
against any decent citizen
resolved to stand up for law, order,
everyday commonsense,
though as likely to receive rough justice
from the law courts as back streets…
(Does anyone really care any more?)
The knives - and guns - are out…
no wonder few are willing to be seen
telling what they think, heard, saw
(more the shame, the cruelty and pity);

And what do the mayor and PM make
of all this? Oh, plenty to say, a limitless
supply of token gestures as Londoners
grow anxious for answers

THE LAST LONG HAULER OUT OF E-BAY

Bid for a ticket,
now halfway to heaven;
angels rushing by - no
less anxious than I to see
the end of the line

Looking down, I see
people on hands and knees
in poverty and pain - far
more anxious than I to see
if God's at home

Looking out, I feel
a devil's breath on my face,
smell incense burning
like a pot-pourri of roses
and grow anxious

Bid for a ticket,
now halfway to heaven;
angels rushing past - no
less anxious as I to make up
for lost time

SOUNDING OUT THE STOCK MARKET

Forget stocks, shares and one-upmanship
supposedly winning the day;
no sounder investment than in friendship

Biting fingernails, seeing the Footsie slip,
fall or climb as well it may;
forget stocks, shares, and one-upmanship

The Stock Exchange, it's a high ego trip,
lives made and lost along the way;
no sounder investment than in friendship

Bad choices, to a body's bare bones strip,
no cover even for a rainy day;
forget stocks, shares, and one-upmanship

See a canny streak pass for a treasure ship
where pirates would have their way;
no sounder investment than in friendship

Though into life's temptations we may dip,
let love, not wealth, have the last say;
forget stocks, shares and one-upmanship;
no sounder investment than in friendship

CAUGHT ON CCTV

Men and women, every shape, size, colour,
on the street...
crowding each other, elbowing a passage,
nobody apologizing

Man in a suit, pocket picked by a kid about
fourteen...
woman in a short skirt, fumbled by a guy
getting married soon

Children wanting this and that, parents look
scared to say, 'No!'
cop on the beat, deciding... no pay packet
worth this hassle?

Dark faces and lighter stuck in poems about
racism...
light fingers and darker rewriting byelaws
for drug free zones

Dog dashes in front of a car, tyres screaming,
people crying blue murder...
mutt's okay, runs off, driver doesn't even stop;
a few of us make eye contact

People - all shapes, sizes, colours, lips moving;
street, playing deaf

HOUSE AND GARDEN

At times, memory's door appears to close,
shutting some of us in and others out;
why it should treat us so, nobody knows,
time all but deaf to the heart's lonely shout

It hurts that we can't just pass to and fro
rooms that recall us as we've always been
in a House of Love, each corner we know,
at its windows, sights and scents evergreen

Only now and then the door swings ajar,
allowing us to slip through but awhile
to be as we were and, here at least, are…
as birds on a branch, sure to raise a smile

Should a day come, the door will not open,
be sure nature will tend house and garden

METAMORPHOSIS

Days of nursery rhyme
maturing, breaking free;
mists of time

Learn to talk, walk, climb
this chair, that tree;
days of nursery rhyme

Prone to gene and enzyme
maturing, breaking free;
mists of time

First summits to climb,
marathons run to victory;
days of nursery rhyme

Come to prime,
wandering thoughtfully;
mists of time

Charged with a crime
for each lost opportunity;
days of nursery rhyme,
mists of time

FUNDAMENTALS

Terror on walls, war
in so many words

Beyond understanding,
call the local Council

Catch wrongdoers, let
'em scrub away

Get rid of all the anger
till no one sees

Nice clean brick walls,
feel-good factor

War on walls, terror
in so many words

GAME OVER

Soccer yobs singing in shadows,
drunk on an angry moon;
Wind telling tales in ears of grass;
Sleep, plundering imagination;
Drug addicts shooting down stars,
wishing their lives away;
Spreading fast, Pandora's curse
on wings of a new century;
Love, making pledges it means
to keep (like a feisty politician
on the soap box) yet time after time
to its ghosts we turn, let their past
our present blur, pretend the world
was better then, its Old Man
wore a kinder face

Silence, but a huge, vacant cave,
a sadness second to none;
No shadows here, only darkness,
a bleak baying for the moon
in the head, marking us un-dead,
run from chaos too soon;
No choice but retrace our steps,
treading softly on our fears,
crass imagination falling apart like
an emperor's new clothes;
a fairer nature winging far, far softer
shadows than thought could ever
threaten a few soccer killjoys letting
the side down, blind drunk,
deaf to any dawn chorus

EXTRACTS FROM A PRISON DIARY

A neighbour slipped out to buy bread
and…was shot dead;
Hoodies cheered, one waving a gun
(who's next? Could be anyone)

I thought I knew that hood inside-out
till I heard a devil yell, "Shoot!"
A face in shadow, but I knew the voice;
what happened next, my choice

Mates say guns are a must (gang culture),
a necessary feel-good factor;
Suddenly, blood on my designer shoes;
heads cops win, tails I lose

Emergency sirens blasting at my head,
(Like it was me shot someone dead?)
I knelt by the body and called out a name;
the only answer, howls of shame

I was told to wear a white shirt, black tie
for the funeral, but it was a lie;
What difference if I'm dressed up smart?
Better jeans, hood, a caring heart

Later (crying in cuffs) taken back to prison,
old mates, some hoodies, looking on;
Drugs, booze, skipping school, what matter?
It was my finger on the trigger

The idea of prison hadn't bothered me
(I'd seen cool shows on TV);
the reality? I am as meat in a lion's den
only…torn to pieces by men

Oh, to be a school kid again, a wiser one,
who would never carry a gun…
nor would I mistake everyday life for dull,
but get an education, enjoy it to the full

Like bile on the tongue, every word written
for tears and fears I keep well hidden
or drown in each lonely day's angry swell
crashing down on this, my life, my cell

Note: I was asked to write a poem about gun culture by a teacher concerned about its apparent rise in her local area, with a view to its encouraging debate.

MAKING A START

Up to the ears in debt,
a broken romance,
P45 on a table obscuring
newspaper headlines
on war or famine, floods,
earthquakes probably
down to climate change
but no ozone hole
to blame for street crime,
racism, homophobia,
beggars in shop doorways,
children running riot
in supermarkets because
parents afraid to say
no, stop, don't, mustn't
or you'll grow up with
precious few social skills
and even less hope
of getting parole halfway
into a life sentence

Must start to get real, nurture
for a better world

JUST ANOTHER DAY IN THE TERROR BUSINESS

Thinking a song, can't quite recall
how it goes...
no care in the world, except having
overstayed the visa

Good job, future, youth, making all
the right moves;
station, steps, barrier, platform, train,
in everyday sequence

Suddenly, yells, gunshots ringing out,
a dead passenger;
(too late, excuses at press conferences,
conditional apologies)

We can but learn by our mistakes, let
live or die...
(ascribed to Methuselah, perfect model
for a Met police chief?)

Small change, a family's grief in global
economics, mapped out
by politicians, invested in by religions,
held to account by arms dealers

God's gravy train, shunted into a siding
for an overhaul;
maintenance workers told, anything goes
to restore public confidence

[London UK, summer 2005; see endnote xiii].

JOHN BULL'S MIDNIGHT GARDEN

Blades of grass dipped in moonlight,
Old Man winking mischievously
at shadows chasing their own tails
across number ten's garden;
Lights in a window peeking between
chinks in closed curtains, envious
of a night left in peace to play without
fear of interruption

Beyond the wall, a screech of tyres
leaves someone's child dead,
wearing pretty ribbons of moonlight
dipped in a druggie's blood;
Old Man pointing the finger of blame
at shadows chasing their own tails
from the garden of number ten,
preferring to be left in peace without
fear of interruption

Behind the Rehab Centre, closed down
because of local residents objecting,
a desperate company sniffing, injecting,
clutching at straws in a sea of moonlight
flooding the garden of number ten;
Old Man takes to hiding behind clouds
rather than watch shadows made to chase
their own tails where no peace without
fear of interruption

A CRYING SHAME

There are muddy handprints on a gate
that groans as it swings in the wind;
footprints on a path lead to broken steps
rising to a weepy front door pleading
to be opened; children at play may well
ring its dirty pushbutton bell, only
to scream and run away...

The old house is haunted, neighbours say
since the gruesome discovery made
of an old woman who lay dead in her bed
for more than a year, no one to shed
a tear or so much as notice her gone from
the daily round of shopping, washing...
regularly weeding, hedge trimming, going
about her own business like a ghost, less
inclined to socialize than most nor (exactly)
ostracized for this but, even so...
not considered a neighbourly thing to do;
small wonder these good people chose
to moan amongst each other about grimy
windows, disgrace of a garden, an odour
of decaying things dumped and left rotting
in weeds grown tall and spreading until
everyone complaining, wondering what's
got into the old girl, high time someone
paid a call...

A good turnout at the funeral

HURT PRIDE

A gun to my temple, pinned to the floor,
called names, told I'm sick because I'm gay;
frightened for my life and (much) more,
I spoke the words they told me to say

To be gay's a sin, made to cry aloud
for stars, moon, sleepers safe in bed to hear;
kicking at me for walking proud - but
lying to these thugs, I could not bear

Shoot me if you must, whatever, I hissed,
all identity under threat - body, heart and soul;
at least I needed no gun to speak for me,
(no coward, love, its promise will fulfil)

Their pride hurt for my retracting self-denial,
I took heart from heaven's healing smile

THE RHETORIC OF SEPARATISM

Some declare us sick
who are gay, only sure cure
by way of this religion
or that, obeying laws written
in Holy Books, reserving
our own customised prayer
mat in Heaven

I decline the way
of bigots and zealots, reply
that I am happy as I am
nor do I feel any shame
in the way Mother Nature
writes my name

Some place us beyond
the pale who are gay, only
salvation by capitalizing
on society's preferred option
and if sexuality still
won't conform, it can
at least be discreet

I decline the way
of bigots and zealots, reply
that I am happy as I am
nor do I feel any shame
in the way Mother Nature
writes my name

Man's poetry and prose but empty
that fails a common humanity

A PREDATORY LIFE

Anonymous features staring at me
from a hood streaked with mud,
tongue, licking full lips of a wannabe
predator, wet and red…like blood

He bares fine teeth but it is a knife
in one hand that traps my feet
as I brace myself to fight for dear life,
see the boy-predator taste defeat

A second hood approaches, harsh voice
goading its comrade relentlessly
to grab my cash, phone, whatever else
of any value I might carry on me

Now sirens shrieking, both thugs run,
sure to make a killing soon

POOR SPARROW

Once a village, quickly became a town;
green fields, now a housing estate
where we lowered poor sparrow down

In lanes we'd watch the harvest sown,
now highways, commuters running late;
once a village, quickly became a town

Of daisies a tree nymph's spring gown
within creak, squeak, of a trellis gate
where we lowered poor sparrow down

More peace and quiet than ever known,
though small politics its fishwives berate;
once a village, quickly became a town

Office blocks where kites once flown,
nature's finest gone for cheapskate
where we lowered poor sparrow down

Long years past, we children grown,
memories like sunlight on wet roof slate;
once a village, quickly became a town
where we lowered poor sparrow down

SUGGESTIONS

They suggest we try and save garden creatures
and ocean whales before it's too late

They suggest our luxury choices are sure to leave
the generation of 3000 with none

They suggest parents are scared of their children
and raising monsters

They suggest religious leaders pay more attention
to compassion than division

They suggest politicians aren't listening to those
who put them there

They suggest our multicultural societies are failing
themselves and each other

They suggest we start learning the lessons wars
should have taught us

They suggest we're but living will and testament
of a dying planet

So who are they, daring to suggest humankind look
to its shortcomings?

Among leafy choirs, anxious waves, our children
rehearse this world's passing

PART 7

A KINDNESS OF GHOSTS

A KINDNESS OF GHOSTS

Seabirds, making
graceful flight;
Missiles, closing in
on us

Homeowners striving
for a good tan;
Refugees having to settle
for staying alive

Jagged rocks along
the seashore;
Spent shells among
daisies on a lawn

Children crying - for
lost sandcastles?
World, weeping at
mass graves

Climate change across
land, sea and air;
Nature, despairing at
our despair

Love, hope and peace
but as ghosts…
kept busy haunting our
better selves

PROOF OF LIFE
(For Sarah H.)

When people ask who I am,
I tell them to look within themselves
and to each other, perhaps
uncover those mysteries that haunt us
as we journey through life;
How came we here, why, going where?
Questions on the lips, reason
at the inner ear brooking yet more,
answers found wanting

When people ask who I am
I tell them to look around, take in all
they see, feel, need to explain,
justify or change (but how?) perhaps
expecting me to provide
the cure for a sick world, solutions
to its failing societies,
religions losing sight of a vocation
to reunite whom they divide

When people ask who I am,
I tell them to learn the body language
of family, friends, workmates
in the staff room, complete strangers
at bus stops, commuters on trains,
probe those subtle discrepancies between
what we say and what we mean;
stop playing a political correctness game,
give truth its proper name

Who am I? I am the philosopher
that defines who *you* are

IN BLACK SATIN

At the end of the day
darkness wraps us in black satin
and (if we're lucky) takes us
to bed and tucks us in

At the end of the day,
darkness cloaks us in black satin
and (if we're lucky) keeps
the cold at bay

At the end of the day,
darkness hoods us in black satin
and (if we're lucky) a sandman
helps us see

At the end of the day,
darkness hides us in black satin
and (if we're lucky) dawn
means us no harm

At the end of the day,
we can but trust in black satin
to keep our darker selves
under wraps

At the end of the day,
darkness buries us in black satin
and (if we're lucky) leaves us
to rest in peace

EVERY POEM BEGS A STORY

Every poem begs a story from nature
of its power, glory, even shame,
whatever inspires, fuels high fires
of creativity; smouldering coals
in the secret cavities of a soul bound
by natural laws to burst into flames
now and then, if but to light up minds,
expose a heart's needs, its strengths
as well as weaknesses native to a man
or woman's power to love, lust,
hate, even shame a world repeating
its worst over and over again…
leaving poor humanity to follow on
as best it can, strive to put right
its worst wrongs, conveniently rewrite
the saddest songs of war, disasters,
wounds no one expects to heal - with
lines even a paralysed heart can feel
though it take a while yet to penetrate
its body armour or even wake up our
latest United Nations resolution to its
promises of aid on the way, hopes
fading at each long day's turning into
night, night to day, few people
any the wiser for having God's elected
say, 'Let's pray.' As for those…
how many dare stand and be counted
among infants with HIV-AIDS
instead of pontificating on an everyday
morality of sorts?

Every poem begs a story from nature
about responsibility and nurture

EXTRACT FROM A POET'S AUTOBIOGRAPHY

Now among friends, now left alone,
wandering blindly a lonely byway,
thorns like vampires in fields of stone
under a jaundiced sky fast turning grey

No one in sight, man, woman or child,
gargoyles on heaven's outer walls
perpetuating my horror though beguiled
by such hideousness, even as it appals

Tearing at cloth ears, misery and pain
for the end of a world still enduring
Man's rape for the sake of power's gain,
now at Earth Mother's final reckoning

How many poets, I dared wonder aloud,
have permitted demons to spawn here
this fine company of gargoyles, allowed
but a grimace, neither voice nor tear?

Oh for just one kiss of sun on the face,
or garden smells after downpours,
to empathize with a lark's winged grace,
speak out against the world's eyesores

Suddenly, the ghastly mirage was gone,
I was back on track, among old friends
whose loyalty and love I shall lean upon
at the spot where it's said the track ends

WHAT'S IN A NAME?

Call me what you will, I mean well
though my better intentions mistaken
for misguided interference in the ways
of man, woman and child. Navigator
rather than manipulator am I, ready
to guide, lead, through a maze of super
highways, slip roads, dirt tracks, though
suspected of conspiring with nature
against civilization

Call me what you will, I mean well
though my better intentions mistaken
for confrontation with man, woman
and child over some trespass or other
against commandments written in stone
by those rewriting to their own design,
crossing humanity's thin red line, ready
at all times to point the finger of blame
in my direction

Call me what you will, I mean well
though my better intentions mistaken
for retribution, sporting with fragile
emotions, playing false at devotions,
wrecking the well laid plans of mice
and men without so much as giving
any explanation, feeding on the likes
of faith, hope and charity to sustain
an enduring loyalty

Call me what you will, I mean well
whatever G-O-D made to spell

A SPRING CLEANING

At a plain, dull, window,
painting pictures on the sky, brushes
dipped in a prism of unshed tears;
fragments of dreams coming together
with shades of memory, wishful thinking,
multifarious emotion inevitably suppressed
by a stiff-upper-lip culture. No tears, only colour
and shapes spread across a dirty-white ground,
nor the slightest sound, only a heavenly graffiti
speaking out, bringing home to an unquiet heart
hidden meanings for the seeking, finding, learning
about passion's art given free rein, unrestrained
by any need to escape misinterpretation, risk
exposure for all we are, rather than all we would be,
able to see for once, albeit briefly, what's denied
the comfort of memory because the heart has lied
to the soul (and always will?) leaving us to scrawl
our secret lives on heaven's door, hoping, perhaps,
some passing angel might pause to read, pass on
its reflections, hint at solutions, revive our hopes,
give some meaning to survival in a world as bleak
as a wintry sky, now come alive with reds, greens,
blues, pinks, yellows, purples, wishing peace
to all divided peoples, religions left feeding
on contradictions of wealth and power
by voices of a common mind to wipe over
a window, sweep heaven clear

AMONG WOLVES

At the edge of eternity, a wolf
chasing sheep;
At the edge of serendipity, sheep
drop exhausted

At the edge of conscience, wolf
targets a woolly back;
At the edge of history, strong
dominates weak

At the edge of dreams, the weak
put up a fight;
At the edge of darkness, a glimmer
of light

At the edge of our integrity, sheep
left to freefall;
At the edge of its history, wolves
leaping a Black Hole

At the edge of our memory, lambs
sent to slaughter;
At the edge of our bed, a wolf
in sheep's clothing

BEYOND CHRISTMAS

If Christmastide rarely seen to bring joy
or peace to all parts of a troubled world,
let us reflect, each man, woman, girl, boy,
beyond its star, stable, wise men and Word

Though colour, sex, sexuality, creed…
tell dark tales, many beautiful as well,
of peace and joy, love's fulfilling a need
that in each of us seeks a place to dwell

If death, like sickness, knows no boundaries,
war stay deaf to our cries for peace and joy,
let love write the most beautiful stories,
bring hope to each man, woman, girl and boy

To colour, sex, sexuality, creed…
a joy and peace in love, where all faiths feed

LISTEN WITH MOTHER

Listening, she and I, to a mad world
making history

Commuters, shoppers, trick cyclists,
all out to beat the clock

Muggers, pickpockets, rogue hoodies
targeting old ladies

Says a prayer for loved-ones spat on
in our courtrooms

Wonders aloud why, surely, no spring
so cold and bleak?

Yet…claps her hands, laughs, mimics
the first cuckoo in my ear

Proves it just isn't true that no one hears
nightingales any more

Tells fairy stories with happy endings
to kids with HIV-AIDS

Remarks how grey the landscape where
once green fields

Sings lullabies to frail tree spirits made
homeless in old age

Never a life more lived or, even in death,
a voice more loved

THE GUARDIANS

Sentinel of times past, guardian-protector,
Scarborough's castle at the turn of its bays
keeps vigil on the town like a zealous lover

Of battles, banquets, hear its walls murmur,
rage, grieve, yearn… for halcyon days;
sentinel of times past, guardian-protector,

Nearby, the uplifting spirit of a great writer
lends grace to a modern world's ways,
keeps vigil on the town like zealous lover

Brave nautical eye of a veteran godfather
watches out at night for harbour strays;
sentinel of times past, guardian-protector

Earth Mother, bidding heaven come nearer
as pools of light on the sand drop away,
keeps vigil on the town like a zealous lover

As sea to sand, a community come together,
so Time, humanity's present terror allays;
sentinel of times past, guardian-protector,
keep vigil on the town like a zealous lover

[Scarborough, North Yorkshire, March 2007]

LAST EXIT TO EREWHON

Seems everyone has his or her life on track;
feeling so alone that even reaching out for God
seems a waste of time; heartbeat fallen away
like a piece of litter in a gutter left for the street
sweeper. Ah, but let's show the world a smile
even while surfing despair, looking out for that
someone who's never there any more with
open arms to reassure us everything will come
right, we'll see, if a long, long way to go yet.
Then, what? Battle eventually done, and who's
to say who's won in a Hollywood heaven
with more time for its pets than regrets promoted
by daily newspapers, Internet, TV, cinema…
fuel for ratings; everybody love a sob story,
the sadder the better, leaves us feeling marginally
less failed in ourselves, if even more so in
each other, dog paddling, come hell at high water,
to show the neighbours we're holding our own,
everyone high on a quick fix of Happy-Ever-After
fiction meant to keep our children quiet while
we're busy devising an escape route, before those
same beasties we spawned and shoved under
our beds reach their own conclusions, break out,
lay siege to humanity, forcing its hand, lifting
heads from sand to focus on endgame, give blame
its proper name, agree a truce - or its whitewash
walls seen to crumble in ruins, beasties attempting
to feed on bones already stripped bare, nothing
left to show we were here, or so it seems, although
a north wind piling ice on our dreams last heard
carrying a fierce echo, 'I'm here, where are you?'

IN DESPAIR

Sinking darker, lower
than a storm, killing off light,
spreading apprehension;
As muddy water to blocked
drains, filling the senses
till they overflow, no place
to run but flood each path
we'd tread were we not
so weary of dead-ends;
Against earth's risen waters
who stands to win that cannot
even call on heaven to save
its drowning children?
No time to clutch at straws
(been there, done that, spewed
on the tee shirt); faces turned
to walls stained with tears,
vulnerable to Trojan horses;
Naked, returning to the womb
what little it ever gave, save
to bring life, love, hope, joy…
and where are they now
(in these dark days) that made
this world a kinder place?
Piling scorn on that fragile grace
to which it was born

Leave love sleeping as we despair
or dare wake to let it find us there?

HOPE IS A WOMAN

To Mother Nature we bared all
before we were even born
and since then, for good or ill,
her colours worn;
Green, the grass defying acid rain;
Blue, clear skies turning
a blind eye to our obsession
with temporal gain;
Red, streaks of blood across a sky
like the throat of a fox
as the first hound's claw digs in
and darkness falls;
Yellow, the sun's weeping wounds
over drought and famine,
and an outing of inhumanity
on prime time television;
Black, stumps where once we stood
listening to a pretty wood
but did not hear a word it said
and now…all but dead;
Grey, the tearful faces of a next
generation looking down,
baring terror, blaming us even
before they are born

If humankind its lessons learn before
too late, to Earth Mother dare we turn
that, even at Armageddon, she might
stay an old enemy's execution, give us
time to make reparation?

FAIRYTALES ARE AN ENDANGERED SPECIES

Forests, a kaleidoscope
of colour, patterns ever changing
even as we look, like pages
in a child's book bringing fairytales
to life for us

Six swans, six brothers,
winging spring skies, seeking an end
to enchantment but must wait
until their sister, like us, finds a way
to make the change

Knights in armour, wielding
swords that spark a summer sunshine;
rose petals dripping the blood
of rivals challenged and taken to task
for the sake of winning

Snow White in a glass coffin,
no hope of resurrection, the wicked
witch has won? Our turn to woo
the mirror now, autumn skies exposing
a festering of wounds

Dragons, breathing fire
that would kill off the trees to please
property developers who
have no time for fairy tales - or
the likes of us

Twenty-first century knights, wielding
words that spark a wintry sunshine,
robins dripping the blood
of rivals arguing over the last prize left
to us (a glacier coffin?)

LOOKING FOR AFRICA

Living trees, felled
to the ground

Living souls, fallen
in the sun

Dead loss, sweeping
up leaves

Dead eyes, looking
for God

GHOST FINGERS

Inspiring the young, comforting old,
fuelling tales at cosy fires,
melting a frost on cobbles of despair,
thawing the icy grip of fear;
Yet, a warning too or at least a hint
of what's to be, rooted in
shifting sands of a memory playing
fast and loose with our desires,
heavenly spires secretly tumbling us

Partying the young, partnering old,
fireflies dashing at twilight,
breaking into its pregnant silences,
fracturing cruel thoughts;
Yet, an intruder too, wearing a mask
that's oozing familiarity,
shifting sands of a memory playing
fast and loose with our desires,
heavenly spires overtly spinning us

Driving the young, steering the old,
taking rough with smooth,
making inroads to forbidden places,
bringing hope, love;
Yet, a stranger at the wheel, no map
to dictate our route across
shifting sands of memory playing
fast and loose with our desires,
heavenly spires playfully teasing us

Feeding imagination, art's finer promise;
clouds, like ghost fingers, signing to us

PARTY TRICKS

Mourners in a churchyard looking sombre and worn;
bird singing cheerfully in a nearby tree

Sun's rays barely holding out against a rising storm;
spring indifferent to our expectations

Priest intones a ritual as people toss dirt and flowers
into a yawning chasm playing host to it all

Mortality's favourite party tricks going unchallenged;
home truths playing fast and loose with delusion

Body in a box whispering at the ear, "Why am I left
in the dark, surely deserving answers?"

Memory's kinder nature risen to the occasion, despite
dirt and flowers askew on a handsome coffin

(Better to rest in peace than unlikely to save a world
struggling for balance on an axis of evil?)

Mourners in a churchyard looking sombre and worn,
wondering how much a decent funeral costs?

Bird singing cheerfully in a nearby tree while nature's
handsome profile clouds over, aghast

HANDFULS OF DUST

Reaching for the stars,
only in lonely hours;
Reaching for the moon,
only for hope gone

Reaching for a rainbow,
only in sorrow;
Reaching for sunbeams,
only in daydreams

Reaching to pluck clouds
from the sky
only making us cry

Reaching to pluck birds
from the trees;
only songs on a breeze

Reaching out to people
in the street;
only sound, running feet

Reaching for imagination,
if only motivation…
Reaching for redemption,
if only for salvation

Reaching for handfuls of dust;
only love, a must;
Reaching for God's heaven,
if only…

LIVING WITH GHOSTS

I glimpsed a ghost
in spring leaves,
a fragile thing, flickering
with loss and pain
till joy, its brighter light.
bursts through - winter
woods alive again

I glimpsed a ghost
in summer leaves
a bold thing, enjoying
no finer freedom
than hope, a brighter light
bursting through - green
woods strong again

I glimpsed a ghost
in autumn leaves,
such a pretty thing, high
on colourful passions
like home fires acting out
our lives like mummers
in a play

I glimpsed a ghost
in winter snow,
a sad thing, its sorrow
shining through…
yet love, a brighter light
still, watching over
my grave

AMONG SLAVES

I am that breath of wind in the hair
inviting the human spirit to confess
its foibles, rise above its troubles,
show the world what it's made of
though its back forced against a wall,
those vultures, prejudice and fear,
homing in to pick clean the bones of
fathers, mothers, sisters and brothers
lured by false witness here

I am that first kiss of rain on the face,
drawing on the human spirit to open
its heart as a flower its petals to the sky,
lend its beauty to the eye so we do not
pass by but pause to reflect on the how
and why of its being, and ours, reasons
to deny the vultures a victory, let nature
tell a story bitter-sweet of humanity's
attempts to compete

I am that first angry tug at the sleeve
urging the human spirit to turn away
from its prejudices and fears, confront
our lesser selves head-on and expose
them for what they are, though it test us
the more by far...take people as we find,
respecting their privacy, acknowledging
their integrity, learning from a natural
ingenuity to survive

Among slaves of time, I am eyes and ears
who call me Freedom and wipe my tears

SPRING SUNSHINE

Oh, for spring's leafy corner of the heart
where I love to lie and watch the sunrise,
a beacon of hope to guide us at the start
of life-shadows playing tricks on our eyes

Each time a cloud passes over my head
they home in on me, such shadows, on wing
like birds of prey demanding to be fed
or winter dreams grown impatient for spring

Clouds pass, leafy sky fills with song again
come the sun at noon and twilight's descent;
though shadows chill a heart like winter rain,
in one corner, spring sunshine never spent

Should shadows swoop and carry me away,
find love's leafy corner, spring sure to stay

APPENDIX I

WELCOME TO THE 21st CENTURY

Space probes in the galaxy,
harbingers of the Mars tourist;
24/7 banking on the Internet
(oops, beware a virus);
Violence on the streets, now
an everyday occurrence;
Drivers still using mobiles
at the wheel, refusing to believe
calling - or drinking - can kill.
(Besides, the chances are it will
be someone else who dies
and repentance always
goes down well with juries);
New legislation in the UK - to
make sure burglars are ok;
Meanwhile, people dying trying
to protect their own. Even so,
let's keep a sense of proportion,
a limit to self-defence
(or anarchy?) and what, pray,
have our politicians to say
about this? Not a lot…unless
an election round the next corner
then anything goes, if only to
pull the punters in on polling day
(or catch us out, as the case
may be). And how does religion
fit in with our daily lives?
Still preaching stories about peace
and loving our neighbours…
No matter, suspicion everywhere

we look - but how can we blame
our world leaders for that,
let alone bring them to book?
Dog fights dog, chases cat - and
always will, it's only natural,
like straight talking family values,
paying lip service to gay issues,
insisting women have equality
with men (except on the pay slip
they take home)

Oh, and God save the Economy!

Or, whatever it takes to keep up
appearances - no matter how many
arms and other shady dealings
going on in the name of liberation
and world fraternity

Welcome to the 21st century

Note: An error appears (line21) in this poem in my previous collection, *A Feeling For The Quickness Of Time*. - RNT

APPENDIX 2

THE L-WORD
(For Bob & Bernie)

L-ove is a mystery
above all things,
ecstasy or misery

Poor though we be
or walk among kings,
L-ove is a mystery

Who can say, see
to whom life brings
ecstasy or misery?

Around earth's history
running rings,
L-ove is a mystery

Sharing heaven's glory,
like a bird that sings,
ecstasy or misery

The one eternity
of life's mixed blessings,
L-ove is a mystery,
ecstasy or misery

Note: The title of this poem appears incorrectly in my previous collection, *A Feeling For The Quickness Of Time*.

[i] OUTCOME is a gay self-support group to whom I read poems now and then.

[ii] Stuart is a friend who lives in the lovely Cumbrian countryside near Wigton.

[iii] Joyce is a former mayor of Southall who now lives in Whitstable. The mother of an old friend, I have known her for many years. I also knew her late husband, Charles, and am delighted to include him in this dedication.

[iv] Malcolm was a leading light in the London Borough of Camden's Local History & Archives library for many years. We worked in the same building and enjoyed many chats. He has recently retired.

[v] Auntie Bridie also writes poetry and is someone for whom I have great respect and affection.

[vi] Liam is a fellow [American] poet with whom I have kept in touch since getting to know on the Internet in the late 1990's.

[vii] Angie and Dan were my Good Samaritans. The incident portrayed in the poem is autobiographical.

[viii] Amy is a friend who has shown admirable courage and determination in rising above personal adversity as well as making a good recovery following a brain haemorrhage.

[ix] I first got to know Mike and Trevor on the Internet; they live in Whitby, North Yorkshire.

[x] I first met Brian when he was a co-ordinator for the Outcome group (see above).

[xi] I got to know Gary and Michael on the Internet. They had a civil ceremony last year (2006) and I wish them much happiness in their life together.

[xii] A staff member in a Somerfield store in Kentish Town, October 2006, accused me of shoplifting. Head Office later offered an apology and £50 compensation but I declined, pointing out that it did not reflect either the gravity of the incident or distress caused.

[xiii] On July 22nd 2005, Jean Charles de Menezes, a 27 year-old Brazilian man, was shot seven times in the head at Stockwell Tube station in south London by police who mistakenly thought he was a suicide bomber.

[xiv] Sarah is a friend and former library colleague who lives with her husband and two children in Chesham (Bucks).

ABOUT THE POET:

Roger N. Taber was born in December 1945 and graduated from the University of Kent in Canterbury, [UK] in1973. A librarian by profession, he now lives in London. Gay and partially deaf, he is a passionate integrationist and makes a point of including poetry on a gay theme among poems on many other themes in his collections. Some 500+ poems have appeared in various poetry magazines and anthologies worldwide

Contact: rogertab@aol.com